Wallace-Homestead Price Guide to

American *Country* Antiques

12th edition

Wallace-Homestead

PRICE GUIDE TO
AMERICAN
Country
ANTIQUES
12TH EDITION

Don and Carol Raycraft

Wallace-Homestead
Book Company
Radnor, Pennsylvania

Library of Congress Catalog Card Number: 86-640023
ISBN 0-87069-585-1

Designed by Anthony Jacobson
Cover photograph taken by Steve Smedley
Manufactured in the United States of America

1 2 3 4 5 6 7 8 9 0   2 1 0 9 8 7 6 5 4 3

Contents

Acknowledgments

Judy Adams
Judith Anderson
Jon Balke
Joan Barker
David Beier
Tom and Nancy Benda
Gary and Lorraine Boggio
Copake Country Auctions
Teri and Joe Dziadul
Ken and Carlene Elliott
Mike Fallon
Garth's Auctions Inc.
Bernie and Gerry Green
Doug Hamel
Rose Holtzclaw
Alex Hood
Liz Johnson
Edie Lacey
Joy and Robert Luke
Kris Marks
Paul McInnis Inc. Auction Gallery

Carolyn Mock
Pat Newsom
Joe and Opal Pickens
Tom Porter
Vera Porter
Darrell and Lana Potter
Ron and Ann Roop
Carolyn Sanders
Laurie Schoendorfer
Dianne Shubin
Georganne Slapper
Steve and Donna Smedley
Bill Smith
Judy Smith
Dawn Sprout
Jean Strang
Effie Swearingen
Ellen Tatem
Dick and Kay Thompson
Vicki and Bruce Waasdorp
Debbie Yountz

Photography

Carol Raycraft
Jon Balke
David Beier
Tom Benda
Gary Boggio
Joe Dziadul
Sue Jones
Robert Luke

Darrell Potter
R. Craig Raycraft
Dick and Char Schlichting
Steve Smedley
Bill Smith
Dawn Sprout
Ellen Tatem

Introduction

Many remedial students of American history attribute the beginning of the Revolutionary War to some Boston teenagers with time on their hands (the malls were closed) who threw snowballs at nine British soldiers. One of the hated redcoats was returning with a carryout coffee (no sugar, cream) from the McDonalds across the street, saw the commotion, ran to assist his beseiged comrades, slipped on the ice, and accidentally fired his gun. The rest is history.

Remedial students of the evolution of American country antiques collecting can relate to the previous version of history because they are constantly attempting to pinpoint the origins of selected collecting manias and marketing trends. In the 1920s and 1930s it may have been Windsor chairs or handwrought fireplace tools; in the 1940s and 1950s it was refinished "colonial" furniture. The 1960s and 1970s brought a demand for "country" antiques. The 1980s saw a growing interest in finding furniture in its original finish. The early 1990s have seen objects with a painted or "original" finish continuing to hold collectors' interest and rising in value. Usually, there is some spark that ignites interest in a particular item or "look" that quickly excites the collecting masses.

In the early 1970s an article appeared in *Early American Life* magazine that featured the home and various collections of an Ohio antiques dealer. Among many exceptional pieces in her home was an open pine cupboard that was filled with small stacks of pantry boxes in myriad colors. Pantry boxes were cheaply constructed and mass-produced nineteenth-century wooden storage containers with lids. They were usually painted shortly after their purchase because light woods (maple and pine) quickly became stained or discolored through contact with greasy hands, smoky rooms, and daily use. The paint also protected the wood and allowed the housekeeper to differentiate among the several boxes in need of a specific condiment. Typically, the boxes range in diameter from two or three inches to more than eighteen inches.

Prior to the magazine article many collectors occasionally bought painted pantry boxes to set around the house or for storage. A very few farsighted individuals put three or four boxes in a small stack on a table.

Few of us had perceived how a cupboard would look filled with forty pantry boxes in as many variations of color. When we first saw the picture and realized the potential of pantry boxes, it all quickly came together and the possibilities were obvious.

Within a relatively brief period, the simple pantry box with a coat of crudely applied paint that had been priced at $12 to $15 in July was $50 in October. Almost two decades later we seldom see originally painted boxes for less than $200 to $250, and the quality of these boxes is not nearly as high as those that went into collections with the first wave of interest.

Recently a magazine article and a book displayed the seaside home of a well-known actor and his wife. On a patio in the garden was a painted bench randomly covered with galvanized watering cans in a variety of sizes and colors.

A combination of the pictures, word-of-mouth descriptions, and a yearning by many who enjoy the "hunt" to actually be able to find something for a reasonable price resulted in a national mania among country collectors for watering cans.

Cans that would have gone unsold at a garage sale six months previously were now being "seriously" collected for $35 to $95 each depending on the amount of wear and the quality of the "finish." Watering cans with "old" paint were priced at much more than $100. Keep in mind that *old* is a relative term.

Guidelines

If you are going to attempt to anticipate the next piece of Americana that is going to become hot, you might want to consider the information below and check to see that it meets our guidelines.

1. The item is inexpensive *now* and was *originally* inexpensive.

2. It is available but *not* plentiful.

3. It is nondescript when it stands alone. It becomes much more desirable in combination with other examples in a stack, collection, or grouping of similar objects.

4. The finish is original and shows some evidence of wear and use.

5. Generally, the item is utilitarian rather than decorative and factory-made rather than handcrafted.

6. The best examples are always purchased before the majority of collectors realize that the object is even collectible.

7. The collecting fire is started by a picture or article in a country-oriented decorating magazine or coffee table book.

8. Prices escalate dramatically when dealers realize that there is a profit to be made and they start to buy the object wherever it can be found.

9. Prices have already dropped like a rock when most of the antiques malls in Iowa and Idaho have two or three of the items in every booth.

10. Prices have completely bottomed out when you read about what a "fascinating" hobby it is in your local newspaper.

11. When your mother-in-law gives you one for Christmas, it is officially over.

Price Guides

The purpose of any price guide is to provide the reader with a broad appreciation of the approximate value of a given item. A price guide should be used much like an auction catalog that contains an estimation of an item's worth. The auctioneer includes an estimate to help potential bidders gain some perspective about values and a hint about what to expect to pay on auction day.

This particular price guide assumes that the item pictured or described is at least in excellent, original condition and, unless otherwise stated, the value listed reflects that condition.

Each year we contact nationally known dealers, auction houses, and private collectors from diverse geographical sections of the United States to establish values for American country antiques.

Values listed are the approximate prices the items are being offered for in a shop or mall, or the price the piece has brought at auction.

In looking over previous editions of this book, we have noted steadily increasing prices in almost all categories of Americana. Collectors and dealers also have to work much harder each year to find comparable quality goods for resale or for their individual homes.

We also have reported previously that there is growing price consistency for similar pieces of Americana across the entire nation. There are no longer dramatic price differences between Maine and California or Oregon and Illinois, as was the case a decade ago.

1 *Antiques and Collectibles*

The United States Customs Service has the responsibility of placing import duties or taxes on items brought into the United States from other countries. Until 1967 the Customs Service decreed that only if an item was made prior to 1830 could it be classified as an antique; anything made after 1830 was considered to be something other than an antique.

The 1830 line of demarcation separating antiques from collectibles was selected because that date commonly is cited by cultural historians to denote the change from homemade and handmade household goods and furnishings to a factory-made or mechanized method of production.

Since 1967 the Customs Service has perceived an antique to be a minimum of 100 years old. This means that an English tobacco tin mass-produced in 1892 now can enter the

United States as an antique rather than a collectible.

The fact that the item was machine-made rather than crafted by hand is not a factor. Age, rather than the manner in which an object was made, is the single criterion.

Memory Lane

In 1953 the majority of the eleven-year-old scholars who attended Oakland Grade School in Bloomington, Illinois, were collecting baseball cards. We stood in short lines at DeMents' Neighborhood Grocery next to the school grounds or tempted the fates and the powerful paddle of Miss Stewart by illegally leaving the playground over the noon hour and sprinting three blocks to a Piggly Wiggly grocery store where there were cases of Topps and Bowman boxes from which to make our clandestine selections.

Most of us had a nickel that our fathers had provided for an afterschool candy bar, usually a Whiz or Forever Yours, to spend instead of a package of baseball cards. The anticipation of what was in the package that awaited our arrival at the store was always worth the risk of facing Miss Stewart on our return.

We were totally oblivious to the condition of the cards, any monetary values, or the total number of cards that the company produced, but we knew that a Mantle was usually worth at least two Warren Spahns and a Satchel Paige. We were collectors and we had never met another collector who sold cards. We traded cards.

In 1993 the majority of the eleven-year-olds at Oakland Grade School, and their peers across America, will not be interested in putting together a collection of baseball cards to bind with rubber bands and put in a shoebox until they go off to college and their mothers toss them away on a sunny Tuesday morning in early September while they are asleep at a fraternity house 200 miles away. Baseball card collectors of all ages today are stockbrokers watching values rise and fall based on a hitter's home run total or a pitcher's won-lost percentage. There are monthly and even weekly price guides that chart the constantly fluctuating prices.

The point of this brief journey down memory lane is that the baseball-card mentality has permeated the entire field of collectibles.

What's it worth? is the expression of the moment. Objects may or may not have value the day after tomorrow. When Pee Wee Herman found himself at odds with the police in a Florida movie theater, the resulting publicity briefly created a situation where memorabilia with his name or image attached was taken off the discount or sale table and eagerly remarked for the collectors sure to stop by seeking an investment in collectibles.

When the press reported that L'eggs Hosiery's egg-shaped plastic container was going to be discontinued for environmental reasons, "serious" collectors realized that prices could possibly rise and many rushed out to purchase as many containers as possible before the recycled cardboard containers came onto the shelves of local stores.

One of the joys that we have savored in our quest for American country antiques over the years is the opportunity to own a piece of furniture, a decorated stoneware jug, or a quilt that may be unique. There is also some satisfaction secured from speculating about the previous owners of a painted kitchen chair and wondering how it made its way into our possession that can never be secured from the accumulation of fifty L'eggs containers.

Prices

Collectors of American country antiques also are not immune from the fluctuations in prices that face collectibles investors. In the 1970s several national interior design magazines began to promote the country look with articles and, eventually, entire publications filled with lavishly illustrated displays of homes and individual collections of Americana. At that point many new collectors armed with bulging pockets and little knowledge began to enter the marketplace with a specific desire to replicate the contents of a particular room in a specific magazine. If the room had a copper weathervane manufactured by Cushing and White (Waltham, Massachusetts) or E.G. Washburne (Danvers, Massachusetts) in the late nineteenth century, it went to the top of their "want" list.

Dealers attempted to meet the increasing demand for weathervanes and other examples of Americana by filling their shops. Numerous folk art collectors somehow decided that factory-made weathervanes fell within their field of interest and country collectors faced new competition with even deeper pockets.

As the demand for merchandise increased, prices soared. When items that previously sold for a few hundred dollars now had people waiting impatiently in line to pay several thousand dollars, as was the case with weathervanes, skillfully manufactured and artificially aged fakes began to appear occasionally in the windows of renowned dealers and to grace the covers of some auction house catalogs.

Many collectors were convinced that prices would steadily increase and a significant amount of money could be made by purchasing weathervanes.

A portion of the bottom of the weathervane market fell out when questions were raised about the authenticity of some expensive examples sold by major dealers to private collectors. There was a significant amount of negative publicity created by the controversy and the net result was considerably less than positive.

When neophyte collectors are uncertain about the age of the antiques they are considering for purchase, the tendency is not to buy. This uncertainty, coupled with a diminished interest in folk art, took some more collectors out of the hunt for weathervanes.

Remember that over time a great many variables enter into determining the interest we have in a given category of collectibles or antiques and the prices we will pay for them.

2
American Country Antiques 101: The Crash Course

This section is devoted to making you a national authority or at least the most knowledgeable individual you know (if you presently find yourself incarcerated in solitary confinement for a crime you probably committed).

An analogy can be drawn between our mission in this exercise and a medical self-help book. We want you to be able to recognize that you are injured, find the first aid kit, clean the scratch or take out the splinter, and apply the proper bandage without permanently maiming yourself.

We *don't* expect you to be able to give a complete physical examination, recognize symptoms of rare tropical diseases, or write a prescription.

We *do* expect you to be familiar with a limited variety of terms that will allow you to conduct a dialogue with someone who will be under the misapprehension that you are informed.

You will have enough information to be a well-received visiting lecturer at the January meeting of your local antiques study group if the scheduled speaker is unable to appear due to snow-storm, monsoon, a long line at the neighborhood White Castle hamburger outlet, or a schedule change down at the bus station.

In the nineteenth century, hinges, drawer pulls or knobs, and broken chair rungs were replaced just like the light bulb in the closet where Aunt Edna hides the peach brandy. Rarely does a piece of furniture come out of a basement or barn today without a multiplicity of additions and deletions.

It is extremely difficult to find a cupboard, bench, or dry sink that has survived a century of use and abuse without being refinished, repainted, or reworked with varying degrees of success.

In the 1950s and 1960s collectors of primitives routinely stripped pine furniture to get down to the wood.

In the 1970s and 1980s tastes gradually matured and pine furniture with an original painted finish became the collectible of the moment. The painted finish that was earlier removed often was surreptitiously returned on many pieces, and collectors had another variable to ponder when they found something they desired at a show, auction, or in an antiques shop.

It is important that you examine a potential purchase carefully before you write the check. If it is a table, pull out the drawer and note how it is put together, check the underside of the top for any alterations, and look carefully at the legs to see if they have been "pieced out" or had three-to-four inches of height added.

The information that follows will not necessarily provide answers to your questions about the identification and dating of a piece of country furniture, but it will offer some serious clues and open some doors that can be utilized in the process.

Wood Screws

Wood screws used in pieces of furniture made in North America in the 1700s always were hand forged. Eighteenth-century wood screws are distinguished by unevenly spaced threads and irregular (out of round) heads. The heads had narrow and shallow screw-driver slots that were almost always off-center. The ends of the screws were blunt rather than pointed.

By 1825 machine-made screws became available in most urban areas. The shanks or bodies of these screws were much more consistent in size and shape than the earlier handwrought screws. The threads were also evenly spaced. The heads of the factory-made screws from this period were still irregular in shape and contained screwdriver slots that were equally as narrow, shallow, and off-center as the eighteenth-century examples. During this period, the ends of the wood screws were still blunt rather than pointed.

Factory-made screws with sharp or gimlet points were not commonly in use until the early 1870s.

Drawer Pulls

The wooden knobs used on eighteenth- and early nineteenth-century country furniture were usually 3″ to 3½″ long. The shaft of the knob was driven into a hole with a slightly smaller diameter on the front of the door or drawer and held firmly in place by friction. Some of these early knobs had a hand-forged screw placed into the shaft from the back of the drawer front or the door. The knobs held by the screws lasted much longer than the friction-driven knobs, which tended to shrink in size over time and fall out of the hole in the drawer front or door.

Pressed glass knobs mounted on iron posts were popular after 1825 and continued in use until the late nineteenth century.

Mushroom-shaped knobs about 1″ deep and up to 2½″ in diameter were popular from about 1830 until the early 1900s.

The nuts that were attached to the threaded posts to hold the wooden knobs firmly in place sometimes can be used in the dating process. Prior to 1870 the typical nut was irregularly shaped. After the early 1870s, when factory produced nuts and bolts were precision made in huge quantities, the nuts were almost perfectly square or hexagonal (six-sided) in shape.

White porcelain knobs became popular in the 1890s. It is not uncommon to find a cupboard or bedside table from the 1830s with porcelain knobs. Homeowners would often "dress up" a piece of country furniture with porcelain replacement knobs that were readily available at hardware stores or through mail-order catalogs.

Dovetailing

Dovetailing is a cabinetmaker's technique commonly used to join two pieces of wood at a corner. Eighteenth-century craftsmen often used a single large dovetail in each corner to hold a drawer together. Before making the cut

for a dovetail, it was necessary to scratch a vertical line (scribe mark) into the wood at each corner to mark the depth of the cut.

In the late 1880s a dovetailing machine was introduced that simplified the process considerably. Machine-made

Dovetails

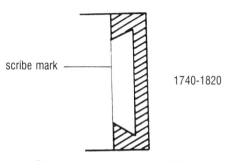

Single large dovetail from the 1700s
to the early 1800s.

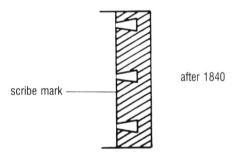

Handcut dovetails from the mid-1800s.

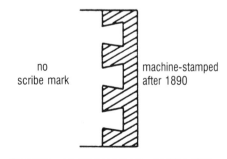

Dovetails were stamped out by machine after 1890. There is no scribe mark because the machine automatically made the cut and did not need a mark.

dovetails are regularly spaced and identical to one another in size and shape. There was no need for a scribe mark when the machine was utilized in the production of furniture.

It is generally safe to assume that if the drawers of a table or cupboard have machine-stamped dovetails, the piece was probably factory-made *after* 1890.

The old and often-quoted rule "The larger and fewer the dovetails, the older the piece" is still accurate.

Nails

Auctioneers love to point out to potential bidders that a particular piece of country furniture contains dovetailed drawers and square nails. As you already know, there are several varieties of dovetails, and the hardware store on the corner still sells square nails for use in masonary projects or building pine cupboards.

You have to assume that the nails used to construct the piece of furniture that you can't live without carried no rust when they were initially hammered into place. Over the years iron nails will rust and the wood that immediately surrounds the nail also will discolor and "rust." This is a natural process; it does not date the piece of furniture but it does tell you that the nail and the wood have been together for years.

If the head of the nail displays signs of rust but the wood around it is clean, the nail and the wood have not been intimate for too long and skepticism should be the mood of the moment about the age of the piece.

Square nails that were machine made were in general use until the 1870s. Machine-made wire nails with round heads, almost identical to those in use today, began to appear on hardware store shelves by the early 1880s.

It is also logical that nineteenth-century cabinetmakers did not rush out and buy the new type of nail as soon as it arrived at the store. Several kegs of square nails that were already on hand in the workshop could have lasted well into the next generation.

Patina

The patina on a piece of furniture can be compared to the face of a beautiful woman. Over time the once fresh and vibrant complexion takes on the wrinkles and blemishes earned through contact with daily life. The basic structure remains the same but the surface quality is slightly altered through the aging process.

For example, a pine board that was almost white when freshly nailed or dovetailed to the back of a six-board blanket chest in 1830 will have darkened considerably by 1900 due to exposure to air, dust, and indirect sunlight. If the unpainted wood was directly exposed to sunlight, it would be even several shades darker over the same period of time.

The inside of the blanket chest rarely comes in contact with sunlight, and those boards tend to remain as white as the day they were joined together.

The patina usually cannot be used to date a piece of furniture or even provide an estimation of age; however, an examination of the patina does provide clues to the overall determination of the age, origin, finish, and value of an item.

During the period of time when country furniture was automatically refinished, shellacked, and waxed, patina was not a factor. In today's marketplace many collectors are vitally interested in finding a piece in its original or "early" finish and are willing to pay a premium for it. This demand has created a satellite industry of skilled fakers who reapply the "old" or "original" finish and dramatically inflate the price tag of the piece.

Basic Don'ts

There is some fundamental knowledge that you must possess. We have listed only a brief sampling. You have so much to learn.

1. Don't ask the antiques mall proprietor how often the dealers show up to repile their booths.

2. Don't ask the dealer if the wart on his nose has been biopsied.

3. Don't ask if there are any "better" shops or malls in the immediate vicinity.

4. Don't ask if the crudely made cupboard in the corner was damaged when it fell off the truck on the way into the shop.

5. Don't stop at any antiques shop where there are more than two abandoned cars jacked up in the front yard.

6. Don't assume that every antiques shop in Maine will have a painted cupboard, and don't assume that every antiques shop in Iowa won't have a painted cupboard.

7. Don't believe the adage that there is a great treasure at a bargain price in every shop or mall, and if you take the time to search, it can belong to you. It's a lie.

8. Don't assume that just because you bought something, someone else will eventually want to buy it from you. You may be one of a kind.

9. Don't hesitate to buy something that you have been looking for at an antiques show or outdoor market if the price is even close to "right." It is a given that if you wait for a "better one," the "right" one will be gone when you finally come back to sign the check.

10. Don't forget your lunch money and don't get in any cars with strangers.

Collecting Pie Safes

1. Unlike some pieces of country furniture, most pie safes had a life after they were replaced by built-in cabinets or pantries for storing food. The safes were initially put on the back porch for extra storage space after the new kitchens were built. Most eventually ended their functional careers in a wet basement or drafty barn before being rescued half a century later by antiques dealers or a passing collector with a weakness for knocking on doors.

2. Safes are usually found with weather-related structural problems. Exposure to water has rusted the tins and decayed the wood. The painted finish has been largely worn away by the elements and the years.

3. Collectors can still find pie safes in quantity. The trick is to find quality safes with the pierced tin panels and a painted surface intact.

4. Most pie safes were made of pine or a combination of poplar and pine. Walnut safes (seldom painted) also are occasionally uncovered, especially in Illinois, Indiana, and Iowa. Factory-made safes of maple or oak with solid doors and circular cutouts on the sides covered with screen wire date after 1900.

5. The tins could be pierced by machine or by hand with a nail and hammer. Most tins have simple geometric designs. More valuable pie safes have names, dates, cities, birds, or animals pierced into the tin panels. The logos of fraternal (Masonic) organizations also have been happened upon by collectors and add much to the desirability of a pie safe. The quality and condition of the tins are major factors in determining the value of a pie safe.

6. Over time, exposure of a pie safe to water in a wet basement usually resulted in severe damage to the legs that necessitated some type of amputation. There should be a minimum distance of six to ten inches from floor level to the body of the safe. If the safe is only two to five inches off the floor, it has probably lost height due to some kind of structural mishap.

Kitchen Pie Safe

Dates: 1840-1900
Wood: pine, pine and poplar, walnut, oak
Finish: Pine and poplar and pine safes always were painted. Walnut safes and factory-made oak safes were typically left unpainted.

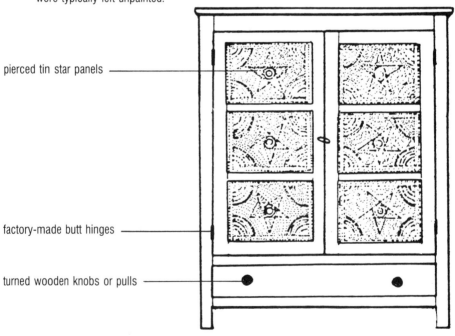

pierced tin star panels

factory-made butt hinges

turned wooden knobs or pulls

14

Collecting Dry Sinks

Dry sinks commonly were used in rural homes without indoor plumbing well into the twentieth century. A dry sink is precisely what its name implies. It contained a well or trough lined with zinc and was used much like a "wet" sink in homes with indoor plumbing. Some of the dry sinks also had a drain in the bottom of the zinc-lined well that allowed water to run into a bucket or into a pipe that sent it outside when the plug was pulled.

A journal kept by a young girl from Chatsworth, Illinois, between 1865 and 1885 contains a description of the dry sink in her home.

The sink stood next to a window on one side of the room. It was a watertight wooden box with cupboards for pots and pans underneath. At one end was the pump that brought the water from the cistern under one corner of the house. The drain pipe from the sink went through the floor and outer wall. The waste water poured out onto the top of the ground that here fortunately sloped away from the house. Those pipes with the one that brought the rainwater from the wooden troughs along the eaves of the roof were the only bits of plumbing on the farm.

1. The dry sink evolved from the earlier bucket bench with the addition of doors and a zinc-lined well or trough. The doors enclosed a storage area.

2. If a dry sink is found with a copper-lined well, it is a recent addition.

Pine Dry Sink

Dates: 1870-early 1900s
Wood: pine, poplar and pine
Finish: always painted

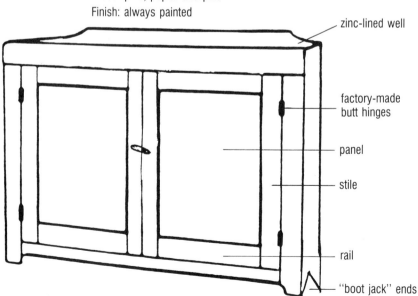

zinc-lined well

factory-made butt hinges

panel

stile

rail

"boot jack" ends

Pine Dry Sink

Dates: 1860-1900
Wood: pine, poplar and pine
Finish: always painted

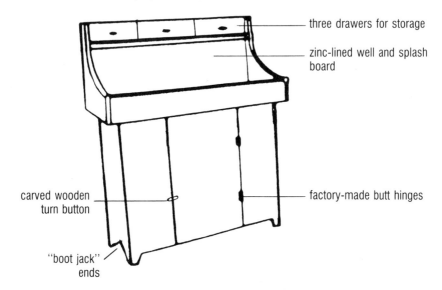

three drawers for storage

zinc-lined well and splash board

carved wooden turn button

factory-made butt hinges

"boot jack" ends

3. Sinks with their original zinc linings intact are uncommon. The original lining usually does not add a great deal to the value of a sink because it is usually in poor repair and has to be taken out anyway.

4. The wooden well area without the zinc lining should show signs of discoloration due to periodic contact with water seeping under the lining.

5. Most dry sinks were made of pine or a combination of pine and poplar. Occasionally a midwestern sink made of walnut or a late factory-made version of oak surfaces. The softwood sinks (pine and poplar) *always* were painted. Check the underside of the sink for a paint history if the piece has been refinished. It is not unusual to find a sink with six to eight coats of paint.

6. Sinks can take several forms. Some later sinks had a lift top over the well that served as a work counter or a cupboard arrangement with a shelf and doors above the well.

7. Sinks constructed between 1880–1920 often were made with commercially produced wainscotting rather than individual boards butted up against one another and nailed to the frame. The tongue-in-groove wainscotting was commonly available at lumberyards after 1880 in most areas of the United States.

3 *Country Store Antiques*

In December 1991 we had a telephone call from a pharmacist who was retiring after working more than forty years in a building that he owned. The original drugstore had opened in 1923.

He wanted us to meet him at his business and go through the building to point out items that may have value to antiques collectors. The shelving and a variety of fixtures had been in place since the store had opened, almost seventy years previously.

If you are even a casual collector of store-related antiques or advertising, this type of invitation can inspire endless speculation about what might be in the attic or the basement. Was it possible that an unopened case of 1952 Topps baseball cards was stacked under the stairs by a careless stockboy while Harry Truman was president?

As it turned out, the tour of the facility and the basement resulted only in the purchase of an Ex-Lax thermometer that had been on the front of the building since Franklin Roosevelt was in the White House. The only other salvageable item of any appreciable age was a safe that was very collectible but also incredibly heavy and almost impossible to separate from the store without removing the roof and importing a crane.

In the 1960s we lived in the rural central Illinois village of Hopedale. There was a surviving general store in the community called Jingling's. Mr. Jingling, the founder of the business, was long deceased by this point but his two elderly daughters, neither of whom had ever married, managed the operation.

As we look back on the situation from our perspective today, our naivete was overshadowed only by our ignorance of the oppportunity that was presented to us.

When Mr. Jingling died, his daughters continued to run the business and rarely, if ever, ordered new merchandise. The store was packed with clothing, hardware, gift items, canned goods, and a wide variety of other goods. Walnut spool cabinets, metal advertising signs, oak needle cases, seed boxes, a huge coffee grinder with a brass American eagle finial, and myriad other store fixtures from the 1920s through 1940s were frozen in time.

It appeared to us that the town and the Jinglings had a unique arrangement. The sisters came to work every morning, closed for an hour at noon, and went home every evening at 5:05 P.M. and were seldom, if ever, bothered by customers. There was no reason to order new merchandise because the old merchandise infrequently went out the door.

As neophyte collectors we failed to grasp the potential of what had been placed before us. We attempted to purchase a spool cabinet, the coffee grinder, and some of the signs, but we were quickly informed that those items were part of the business and not for sale.

We did not take the time to examine the merchandise that was available. Christmas decorations, Halloween items, canned goods, tobacco-related collectibles, and sporting goods were passed over even though they maintained their original price tags from twenty to forty years before.

Several years after we moved from the community and the sisters had either died or entered a nursing home, an auction of the contents of the store drew a large crowd of semi-serious collectors. It should come as no surprise that we found out about the auction three days after it was held.

Demise of the General Store

There were thousands of general stores in the United States, like the Hopedale example described previously, from the 1880s through the 1930s and well into the 1940s. The general stores gradually fell victim to improved "hard" roads and the availability of automobiles to the average family. The hard roads and the automobile allowed small-town and rural Americans the opportunity to travel to larger cities to spend their money.

There was also a growing number of "specialty" stores in the cities that offered many kinds of merchandise that rural general stores could not afford to carry due to space limitations. A wider spectrum of offerings in the specialty stores brought customers from a broader geographic area.

Collecting Country Store Antiques

Many collectors of country store antiques and advertising specialize in a particular category of items. For example, there are numerous collectors interested in the flower and vegetable seed industries. They actively seek packets of garden and flower seeds, seed boxes used for displaying seed packets in stores, seed catalogs, and seed advertising signs and broadsides (paper signs).

Other collectors are attempting to replicate an original country store and want examples of everything that would have been part of an early twentieth-century store. They collect spool cabinets, cast iron coffee grinders, canned goods, display cases, counters, cash registers, signs, and mannequins to display period clothing. They do not want a pack of gum from the 1920s or some cigars from the 1930s. They want unopened boxes in pristine condition.

"Finds"

Periodically an unopened box of tobacco tins that were never used or a stack of 250 tin signs advertising a lumberyard that closed 75 years ago will turn up in the attic of a building scheduled for demolition or in the basement of an abandoned warehouse. The person that discovers the "find" inevitably comes in contact with a dealer who buys everything that was uncovered. In the late 1960s some Dan Patch Cut Plug and Oceanic Cut Plug "lunch box" tobacco tins were found and initially advertised in *The Antique Trader* for $5 to $10 each. Once the tins made their way into the secondary market the price doubled and has done so several times since.

Sources

Collectors of country store antiques typically purchase items at shops, shows, auctions, or through serendipity.

Shops

There are relatively few antiques shops across America that specialize in country store antiques. Many country- or Americana-oriented shops have selected signs, tins, or store fixtures for sale.

It is not uncommon to find a booth or two in an antiques mall where an individual dealer fills a rental space with advertising items.

If dealers are not specialists in country store antiques, their prices tend often to be hit or miss. Some pieces that would be considered rare by a veteran collector may be seriously underpriced, and a paper sign commonly available for $3 to $5 might be priced at $15 to $18.

As is the case with most categories of Americana, dealers whose primary emphasis is in that particular area usually have prices that most accurately reflect the current marketplace.

Auctions

There are several major auction houses that advertise in national hobby publications when conducting sales of country store and advertising antiques and collectibles. The average or beginning collector should at least secure a copy of the catalog and post-sale price list of each auction because there is no better source of information about identification, dating, and current pricing.

Shows

There are a growing number of shows each year that limit dealers to those who specialize in advertising and country store antiques. The dealers who take part are well aware of the value of their merchandise, so there rarely are bargains. Beginning and advanced collectors can expect to view merchandise for sale that they will see nowhere else.

Serendipity

Country store antiques sometimes turn up in unlikely places, giving knowledgeable collectors the opportunity to secure a bargain. Several years ago we stopped for no apparent reason at a yard sale in a rural Indiana village. The homeowner was going into a nursing home and her children were disposing of excess furnishings. Among the assorted pots, pans, and dust mops was a three paneled "stand up" advertising cigarettes with a baseball background in almost pristine condition. We have seen only one other since and it was priced at $1200. This example was $15. The eldest daughter explained that her parents owned a cafe in the village and the sign was so large that her father brought it home and put it in the basement forty years earlier. It had rested in that spot until the garage sale.

Ezra Williams seed box, unusual small size, 9" wide × 4" high × 5" deep. **$275–$350**

Mid-nineteenth-century seed box, painted green, S.B. Noble Garden Seeds. **$150–$175**

Slade's Pure Mustard counter display box. **$150–$160**

Rare Shaker seed box from Mt. Lebanon, N.Y., with interior and exterior labels. **$3000–$3500**

Stickney and Poor's Mustard box. **$150–$160**

E. B. Millar & Co. Penang Spice box. **$100–$125**

Hiram Sibley & Co. seed box with original seed bundles and packets. **$900–$1100**

Stickney and Poor's Mustard box. **$100–$125**

E. W. Burbank Garden Seeds display box, dated 1906. **$300–$335**

Reliable Seeds counter display box. **$200–$240**

Shaker's Garden Seeds box. **$1200–$1500**

Shakers Genuine Garden Seeds box. **$1100–$1300**

Rice's Seeds box. **$300–$335**

Rice's Seeds box with less colorful label. **$150–$175**

Briggs Brothers seed box. **$300–$335**

Thos. W. Emerson & Co. Northern Grown Seeds display box. **$225–$275**

Budd D. Hawkins Northern Seeds display box. **$300–$335**

Button's Raven Gloss Shoe Dressing box. **$135–$165**

Stickney and Poor's Mustard box without a top. **$60–$70**

Lewis Atwood & Son Seeds display box. **$300–$335**

E. R. Durkee & Co. spices box. **$50–$75**

Hiram Sibley & Co. Seeds display box. **$300–$335**

Philips Choice Vegetable Seeds box. **$325–$350**

White Fawn Biscuit box. **$125–$140**

Somerset Garden Seeds display box, c. mid-nineteenth century. **$250–$275**

Catalog (interior label) of Somerset box showing contents.

Rare Shaker's Seeds box with colorful exterior label. **$1500–$1800**

Cressler's Wild Rose Tooth Powder counter display box with unopened containers. **$275–$300**

Interior label of Shaker seed box showing contents.

Shakers Garden Seeds box, c. 1861. **$1400–$1500**

William Burt pea seed box. **$6–$8**

1912 Seed Book from Fairview Seed Farms.
$25–$30

Betsy Ross Shoe Polish with original unopened contents. **$150–$165**

Frank Miller's Blackings shoe polish box.
$200–$250

Sioux City Seed Co. squash seed packet.
$9–$11

Sioux City Seed Co. tomato seed packet. **$9–$11**

Rice's seed box, oak, early twentieth century. **$100–$125**

Sioux City Seed Co. beet seed packet. **$9–$11**

Metal display rack for packets of garden seeds, complete with original decorative decals. **$700–$900**

Lid from a Dixie Chews molasses candy box with colorful interior label. **$200–$235**

Hirdoo Brand Spices box. **$85–$95**

Painted pine store box for seed samples, c. late nineteenth century. **$150–$185**

Northrup King & Co. seed calendar from 1922. **$75–$85**

Red Ranger cigar box for counter sales. **$50–$65**

Glass jars for storing beet and kale seeds from twentieth-century hardware store. $13–$14 **each**

Glass seed jars, twentieth century. $15–$18 **each**

Seed storage jars with pouring lids, c. 1940s. $20–$30 **each**

Tango Stogies tin. $50–$60

Sure Shot chewing tobacco package. **$20–$28**

Lutz's Frog cigar box. **$50–$65**

Peachey Scrap Chewing Tobacco box with 12 original packets. **$140–$150**

Honest Weight Tobacco package. **$70–$85**

Dixie Kid Cut Plug tobacco package. $120–$130

H. A. Nichols Durham Cigars, Bloomington, Ill. $35–$40

Lead Mine handmade cigars box, Galena, Ill. $50–$60

Mallard Cut Plug tobacco package. $50–$60

Lady Hope cigars box. $65–$75

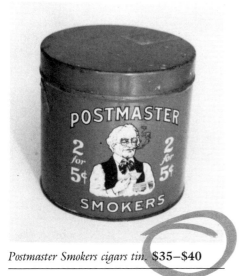

Postmaster Smokers cigars tin. $35–$40

Tuscarora cigar box, Pekin, Ill. $50–$55

Circular cardboard package of Dan Patch Fine Cut tobacco. $65–$75

Unopened Oceanic Cut Plug tobacco package. $25–$30

Three Beauties cigars display box. **$100–$115**

Unopened Huntress Smoking Tobacco package with tax stamp. **$85–$95**

Key West Temptation cigars box. **$100–$125**

Little Tom 5¢ cigars box. **$20–$25**

Green Lucky Strike cigarettes tin. **$35–$45**

Sterling tobacco "tub" or bucket with replaced lid. **$215–$235**

Tennyson cigar counter display. **$100–$130**

T & B cigars counter display. **$100–$115**

Gold Dust washing powder box. **$40–$50**

Silver Cream silver polish box. $40–$45

Turned wooden Carter's Blue Black Fountain Pen Ink container. $50–$55

Turned wooden Carter's Fountain Pen Fluid container. $50–$55

Finck's Overalls paper stand-up. $30–$35

Velvetina Face Powder box. **$20–$25**

Sawyer Biscuit Company animal cracker box. **$25–$28**

Utica Sport Coat box. **$24–$28**

Velvetina Talcum container. **$35–$40**

Box and bottle of Carter's Indelible Ink. **$40–$45**

Cast zinc trade sign clock from a jewelry store, c. 1900. **$375–$500**

Uncle John's Syrup stand-up with rare cane and maple sugar syrup can. **$200–$240**

Partridge Pure Lard can. **$40–$45**

Blue Diamond almond stand-up. **$55–$60**

Betsy Ross Shoe Polish cans. **$25–$28 each**

Corticelli Spool Silk box and contents. **$30–$35**

Fleck's Hoof Packing box. **$30–$35**

Dr. Drake's Croup stand-up. **$175–$185**

Big Smith Shirt cardboard stand-up. **$40–$50**

Buster Brown Mustard can. **$75–$85**

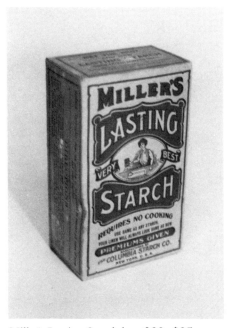

Miller's Lasting Starch box. $30–$35

Dr. Caldwell Syrup Pepsin stand-up. $275–$300

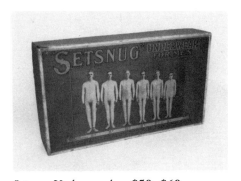

Hoosier Poet Mustard Seed can. $75–$100

Setsnug Underwear box. $50–$60

Smith Brothers Cough Syrup box and unopened bottle. **$35–$50**

Kendall Soapine "The Dirt Killer" box. **$50–$60**

Black Cat Hosiery stand-up. **$15–$20**

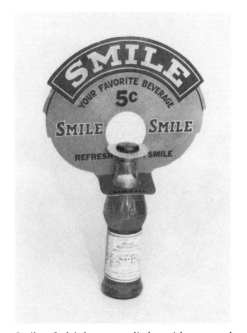

Smile soft drink counter display with unopened bottle. **$50–$60**

Post Toasties Corn Flakes box. $60–$75

Red Kap Work Shirts box. $30–$35

Rare unopened box of Wrigley's Spearmint. $300–$400

F.B. Gates grocery sack. $4–$5

Individual package of Wrigley's Spearmint. $15–$20

Wrigley's Chewing Gum counter display with packages. $60–$65

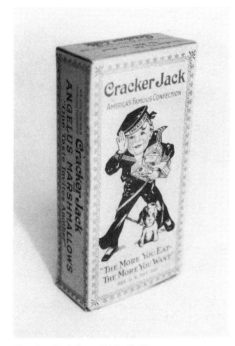

Cracker Jack box. $60–$65

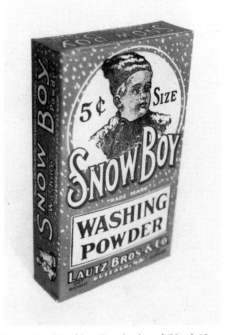

Snow Boy Washing Powder box. $50–$60

Kitchen Klenzer can. $35–$40

Shredded Wheat box. $60–$65

Back side of Shredded Wheat box.

Peacock Coffee container. $50–$60

Golden Robin cinnamon container. $15–$20

Quail Rolled Oats box. **$65–$70**

Robin ginger container. **$20–$25**

Morning Joy Tea container. **$35–$40**

Robin Tea container. **$30–$35**

Gold Medal Hosiery stand-up. **$75–$100**

Rare Underwood Talmage Co. candy tub or bucket. **$550–$750**

Board of Trade Fine Cut tobacco display container. **$400–$600**

Maytag Company oil can with pouring spout. **$100–$135**

Quaker Hominy Grits container. **$30–$35**

Fairy Soap oversized advertising box. **$125–$135**

Pair of shoes, c. 1890–1900. **$65–$70**

Birdseye Sorghum can. **$30–$35**

Butterfinger candy bar box. **$30–$35**

Star Brand Shoes bench. **$350–$400**

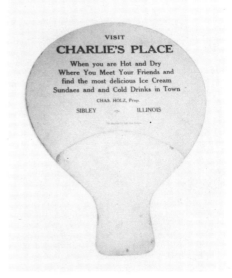

Advertising fan from Charlie's Place, Sibley, Ill.
$15–$20

Back side of fan.

Bars of Lifebuoy and Swan soap. **$8–$10 each**

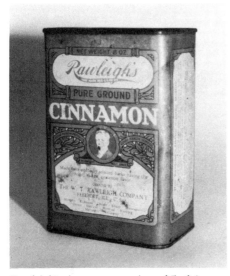

Rawleigh's cinnamon container. **$5–$6**

"Free" Dill's Best pipe cleaners counter display. **$30–$35**

Shaker Pickles bottle with original lid wrapper and lid. **$300–$375**

Shaker horse radish bottle. **$150–$175**

Violet and Burnham Bartlett pears cans. **$4–$7 each**

Cough Cherries store container with slide-out label. **$225–$240**

Dr. C.D. Warner's Blood and Liver Cure pills package and Schenck's Mandrake Liver Pills tin. Package: **$10–$12;** *tin:* **$20–$22**

Headache Wafers box. **$15–$18**

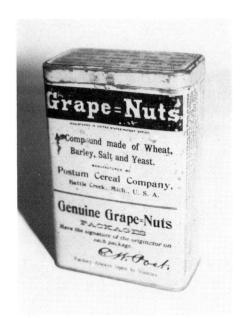

Grape-Nuts tin. **$35–$55**

Top of Grape-Nuts tin.

Cuticura Soap bar. **$2–$3**

Pair of child's shoes. **$35–$40**

Fresh Roasted Coffee bag. $2–$3

Star Bright Coffee bag. $2–$3

4 *Country Furniture*

Most collectors today purchase country furniture from dealers at shows, shops or markets, or at auction. Knocking on doors in rural areas in search of antiques can result in more dog bites and bullet holes than bargains.

Twenty-five years ago there were few collectors searching for pieces of country furniture in their "original" finish. When a piece was found, it was usually safe to assume that it was probably in original condition. Any structural changes had been made years before and were not late additions done to enhance the value or fool the customer.

The supply of cupboards and dry sinks was *greater* than the demand, and prices were fairly stable and always negotiable. As the interest in country furniture gradually grew to exceed the supply of potential purchases in the 1970s and 1980s, prices increased significantly and individual pieces of furniture that were previously considered marginal because of their condition now became highly marketable. From that point on it was almost mandatory that the collector/buyer have some knowledge about what was being purchased.

As prices increased and demand continued to grow, a small minority of dealers found it profitable to employ skilled cabinetmakers and painters to "restore" or "enhance" marginal pieces of country furniture.

To counteract this trend many auction houses and dealers went to great lengths to provide education for their customers. In addition to periodic workshops and seminars, detailed auction catalogs described the furniture to be sold and any changes it may have undergone.

Dealers also provided receipts to their customers that itemized the purchases with accurate information about the age, condition, type of wood, and structural alterations (if any) of the piece. The receipt also served as a warranty or guarantee that the piece was what it was alleged to be.

The increased interest in Americana also spurred the development of magazines like *Country Living* and *Country Home,* which brought additional information to collectors.

Furniture at Auction

Garth's Auctions Inc. of Delaware, Ohio, is one of the nation's best-known sources for Americana sold at auction. Garth's offers detailed and heavily illustrated catalogs for each of their sales by mail and encourages telephone bidding. For $85 per year Garth's will forward a copy of all of its catalogs and a post-sale price list. For $65 collectors specializing in Americana will receive catalogs related to their interest and a post-sale price list for each auction.

All pieces of furniture shown here have been sold at a Garth's auction. Garth's does not charge a buyer's premium.

Information or a subscription can be secured by contacting:

Garth's Auctions Inc.
2690 Stratford Road
Box 369
Delaware, OH 43015
Telephone: (614) 362-4771
Fax: (614) 363-0164

Empire poplar blanket chest with touched-up old worn red paint, turned feet, three dovetailed drawers, replaced hinges, casters, 49" wide × 23" deep × 30¼" high. **$175**

Cherry Empire chest with curly maple and flame-grain cherry veneer facade, four dovetailed drawers with clear blown pulls, 39½" wide × 48½" high. **$750**

Decorated pine immigrant's chest with worn original pale blue paint, stylized floral designs in red panels, 47" wide × 23" deep × 18" high, **$150**; *English pine cupboard with old dark finish and dovetailed case, 23½" wide × 17" deep × 29¼" high,* **$150.**

Primitive pine and poplar mule chest with old worn refinishing, three dovetailed and overlapping drawers and lift lid, 37½" wide × 16¼" deep × 41½" high, **$300;** *ladder-back high chair, refinished and replaced woven splint seat,* **$100.**

Cherry and other hardwood chest of drawers with old worn green paint over red, turned feet, four dovetailed drawers, replaced front feet and turned pulls, 39½" wide × 41" high, **$450;** *small wooden dome-top trunk with faded floral wallpaper covering, 16" long,* **$45.**

Primitive English oak blanket chest with old dark finish, 38½" wide × 14¼" deep × 23" high, $70; ladder-back side chair with graduated slats and turned finials, old worn refinishing, woven splint seat has damage, $50.

Decorated pine and poplar blanket chest with original red graining, dovetailed case and bracket feet, 50" wide × 20¼" deep × 24¼" high, $650; grained footstool with old burnt orange colored repaint and scalloped edge, $35.

Chippendale refinished walnut blanket chest, bracket feet, apron drop, dovetailed case, 46½" wide × 20" deep × 23" high. **$450**

Walnut Chippendale chest with short ogee feet, dovetailed case, brasses are old replacements and three bales are missing, 32½" wide × 41½" high. **$1200**

Painted six-board pine blanket chest with old worn blue repaint over white, repairs to one back foot and hinge rail, 43¼″ × 16½″ × 25″ high, **$375;** *Adirondack-type rocker with old dark brown finish,* **$65.**

Small painted pine chest cleaned down to old blue paint with black on the feet, well-shaped bracket feet, dovetailed case, 38″ wide × 20½″ deep × 23½″ high. **$900**

Sheraton refinished cherry chest with turned legs, paneled ends, four dovetailed drawers, turned pulls, 39½" wide × 44¼" high. **$500**

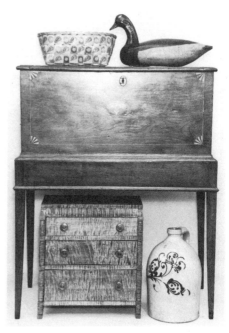

Hepplewhite walnut with inlay sugar chest, square tapered legs, mortised and pinned apron with applied moldings, dovetailed chest with divided interior, old replacement base and old replaced lid that appears to have been cut down to fit chest. **$900**

Poplar bin with red stain, turned feet, dovetailed case with divided interior, and top with lift lid, 27" high × 50" wide × 22" deep. **$350**

Pennsylvania decorated pine blanket chest with original painted decoration, ogee feet and base molding replaced as is till, chest has been cut apart through front dovetails and then reassembled, 50½" wide × 21¼" deep × 25" high. **$400**

Pine chest with old red repaint, cutout feet, well-scalloped front apron, two overlapping drawers with lift lid. **$2550**

Decorated two-piece poplar with worn original reddish-brown flame graining, cutout feet, paneled doors, and one dovetailed drawer in base, 43" wide × 78" high. **$3300**

Two-piece refinished poplar corner cupboard with butternut drawers, simple cutout feet, paneled doors, two dovetailed drawers, and a molded cornice, 83" high × 51½" wide. **$1150**

Poplar corner cupboard with mellow brown re-finishing, top doors are replaced, interior re-painted, back and top have layers of old paint, 46½" wide × 78½" high. **$750**

One-piece poplar corner cupboard with old red paint paneled doors, one dovetailed drawer, 40" wide × 75½" high. **$4600**

One-piece cherry corner cupboard with old refinishing, bracket feet with scalloped apron, replaced cornice. **$4000**

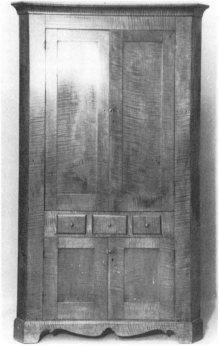

Curly maple corner cupboard with old mellow refinishing, bracket feet, paneled doors, 3 drawers, replaced feet, 45¼" wide × 79½" high. **$2700**

Pair of decorated side chairs with old green over earlier brown with black and gray striping, plank seats and arrow backs. **$245 pair**

Decorated armchair with old yellow repaint, green striping, stenciled and hand-decorated crest, mahogany arms, **$55;** *refinished Hepplewhite cherry and stripe-grained walnut candlestand with spider legs, turned column, one-board top, 16½" diameter × 30" high,* **$360.**

Pair of decorated side chairs, worn original dark graining with stenciled and freehand decoration of peacock foliage scrolls and compote of fruit, one crest with repaired break at splat. **$120 pair**

Continuous arm Windsor chair with splayed base and saddle seat, several repairs and replacements, added iron brace on entire length of bow, spindles are loose, refinished, **$115;** *stand with curly maple base and cherry top, cut corner top is probably older than the base,* **$75.**

Ladder-back armchair with old brown finish, turned arm posts, three slats and turned finials, worn rush seat, **$170;** *poplar dough box with old brown-grained repaint, splayed base with turned legs, dovetailed box and lid,* **$300.**

Unusual pine high chair with stave-constructed barrel-like front and wing back with crest, 43" high, **$65;** *refinished ladder-back high chair with rabbit ear finials and turned arms, new splint seat,* **$110.**

Ladder-back armchair rocker, refinished with a new splint seat, $175; primitive pine apothecary cupboard with old worn refinishing, 8 drawers (with several rebuilt), 39" wide × 14½" deep × 26" high; $550.

Hepplewhite birch candlestand with old worn dark finish over an earlier red, tripod base with spider legs. $275

Windsor armchair with old refinishing, late nineteenth century, $250; Pembroke poplar table with layers of old worn paint, turned legs and drop leaves, $600.

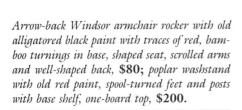

Arrow-back Windsor armchair rocker with old alligatored black paint with traces of red, bamboo turnings in base, shaped seat, scrolled arms and well-shaped back, $80; poplar washstand with old red paint, spool-turned feet and posts with base shelf, one-board top, $200.

Refinished armchair rocker with half-arrow spindles, **$95**; cannonball curly maple and poplar rope bed with worn black finish and replaced side rails, **$425**; child-size armchair with old worn woven cane seat and back, **$125**.

Bow-back Windsor armchair with splayed base, bulbous turnings, "H" stretcher, saddle seat, and heavily alligatored blue repaint that makes repairs hard to spot. **$1000**

Pennsylvania fanback Windsor armchair with old black repaint, splayed base with "H" stretcher, saddle seat. **$1000**

Decorated side chair with original brown paint and black and yellow striping, gilt trim and stenciled fruit and foliage, 32½" high, **$150**; Hepplewhite maple stand with old red paint, two dovetailed drawers, 16¼" × 17" × 28" high, **$1650**.

Queen Anne maple tavern table with some curl, base has old red graining, top has natural finish, **$4900;** *ladder-back hardwood armchair with old red and strong color, old replaced rush seat,* **$2000.**

Bow-back Windsor armchair, splayed base with turned legs and "H" stretcher, worn old red repaint, over earlier green paint, **$950;** *Hepplewhite pine and poplar tavern table cleaned down to worn greenish paint on the base and traces of red on the top,* **$500.**

Refinished curly maple tilt-top tea table with tripod base, turned column with bird cage and round three-board top, nineteenth century, 24" diameter × 26" high. $775

Cherry and other hardwood drop leaf stand with good old red paint, two dovetailed drawers, brass pulls, $1000; set of 6 decorated side chairs, worn original red paint and black graining with yellow striping slat, eagle and crest with foliage, and compote of fruit, $4200 set of 6.

Sheraton refinished curly maple stand with turned legs showing good detail, bowfront dovetailed drawer, and replaced two-board top. **$350**

*Hepplewhite pine and poplar table with original red and black frame graining, square tapered legs, apron with applied edge, one-board top, **$2800**; continuous arm Windsor armchair with old black repaint, splayed base with bulbous turnings, saddle seat, **$850**.*

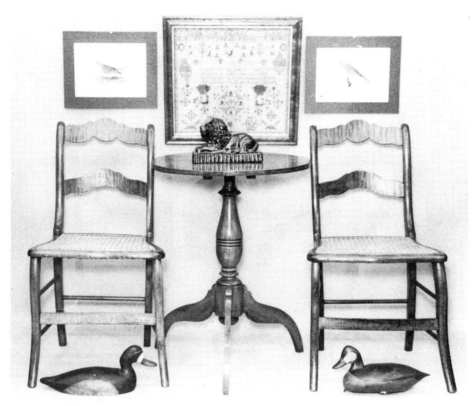

Pair of maple saber-leg side chairs with curl in back slats, old refinishing, and replaced cane seats, **$170 pair;** *refinished curly maple tilt-top table, tripod base with cutout legs, turned column and one-board top,* **$275.**

Hanging pine shelves with old mellow refinishing, scalloped ends, 20" wide × 24" high, **$225;** *ladder-back side chair, hardwood with old red repaint, damaged woven seat,* **$125.**

Sheraton curly maple stand with old dark finish featuring a coat of shiny varnish, turned legs, one-board top and dovetailed drawer, **$700;** *two similar bamboo Windsor side chairs with medallion backs,* **$350 sold as a pair.**

Sheraton poplar table with old varnish finish on base, cleaned two-board top with slight warp and glued repairs, nailed rebuilt drawer, top is either a well-made replacement or a reworked and refastened original. **$175**

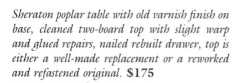

Refinished ladder-back armchair with turned arm supports, four arched slats, and new woven splint seat, **$95**; hanging poplar cupboard with old worn dark graining and dovetailed case, 24½" wide × 35½" high, **$500**.

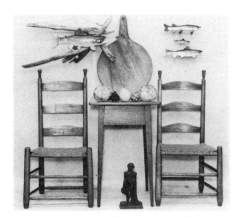

Pair of refinished ladder-back side chairs with turned finials, replaced woven tape seats, traces of old red paint, **$80 pair**; Hepplewhite refinished walnut stand with square tapered legs and one-board top, **$265**.

Decorated pine and walnut washstand with mustard yellow graining on the pine and old dark alligatored finish on the walnut, 29" wide × 21¼" deep × 29½" high, **$250**; decorated Boston rocker, old repaint with stenciled decoration, some repairs, **$45**.

Sheraton refinished curly maple slant-front desk with turned feet, paneled ends, scalloped apron, five overlapping dovetailed drawers, slant-front lid with fitted interior consisting of 12 dovetailed drawers and paneled door, reconstruction made from a chest of drawers, interior reused from another desk, all but the bottom four drawers are old. **$1800**

Refinished maple candlestand, late nineteenth century, 19" diameter × 27½" high. **$85**

Chippendale refinished maple slant-front desk with ogee feet, considerable restoration, lid replaced and interior rebuilt using both new and old drawers, replaced brasses. **$1800**

Poplar water bench with old bluish paint over earlier red paint, one board ends with cutout feet and simple crest rail, 36" wide × 26" high, $425; bamboo Windsor comb-back armchair rocker with old refinishing, pieced repairs in seat and comb has glued repairs, $225.

Pine desk with old brown finish, 2 dovetailed drawers, one front leg has been repaired, 39" wide × 22" deep × 38" high. $275

Yellow pine and poplar stand of primitive construction with worn old dark brown finish, square tapered legs, two drawers and two-board top, $600; Shaker #3 rocking chair with old red varnish finish and stenciled label, damaged woven splint seat, turned finials, $275.

Refinished pine dry sink with one-board door, battens and original cast-iron latch with brass thumb piece, edge damage to gallery, 38" wide × 20½" deep. $350

Hepplewhite poplar sideboard with worn reddish brown finish, replaced hinges on doors, drawer dovetailing that doesn't match, doors and case show signs of some past alterations, 46½" wide × 18½" deep × 43½" high. $110

Pine and poplar decorated jelly cupboard with original red flame graining, one dovetailed drawer, 36¼" wide × 45" high. $1000

Pine crock stand with four curved tier shelves and traces of old blue paint, 44" wide × 50" high, **$400;** *yellow pine pie safe with old worn finish, 12 punched panels, tapered feet,* **$700.**

Poplar jelly cupboard with old red paint, simple cutout feet, paneled doors, and one drawer, 44¼" wide × 15" deep × 60½" high. **$350**

Primitive poplar open pewter cupboard cleaned down to old red paint, cutout feet and paneled door, step-back top, 38" wide × 77½" high. **$1800**

Two-piece poplar wall cupboard with old red finish, dovetailed bracket feet, paneled doors, three dovetailed drawers, 53" wide × 90" high. **$4500**

One-piece pine and poplar step-back wall cupboard with old worn grayish salmon paint, board and batten doors below with double top doors, 43" wide × 73" high, **$505**; wood dome-top trunk with hide covering, leather and tin trim and brass tacks, 24" long, **$150**.

Poplar pie safe taken down to old blue paint, 49½" wide × 47" high, **$500**; poplar box with old red paint, some wear, hasp is missing, 28" long, **$90**.

Pine and poplar hutch table with old mellow refinishing, two-board top with rounded corners, reworked base, 40" wide × 61½" long. **$1100**

Small pine cupboard with old red paint, apparently originally a built-in, 17¼" wide × 36½" high, $550; primitive three-tier crock stand, repairs and green repaint over weathered surface, $250.

One-piece poplar step-back cupboard cleaned down to old red paint with some added black graining, paneled doors in base, cut down slightly from top and top board renailed, 40" wide × 76½" high. $1000

*Hepplewhite pine worktable with old worn brown paint, square tapered legs, mortised and pinned apron and three-board top, 28½" × 55" × 30" high, **$200**; hooked rag rug with geometric design in rich solid colors, 29" high × 44" wide, **$325**.*

*Pine harvest table, old yellow repaint with gold graining, square tapered legs, two-board top, 62½" long × 29" high, **$1000**; doll-size refinished pine chest of drawers with scrolled apron, three large drawers and two smaller drawers, 16" wide × 19" high, **$275**.*

*Hepplewhite pine worktable with oak legs, old worn finish with traces of red paint, square tapered legs, mortised and pinned apron, one overlapping dovetailed drawer, 27½" × 45" × 30" high, **$245**; small mahogany stool with old worn varnish finish, **$25**.*

*Walnut Queen Anne worktable with old refinishing, two dovetailed drawers, breadboard top, restoration includes feet "pieced out," drawers replaced, top is probably a replacement, 33½" × 57½" × 30¼" high. **$400***

Miniature walnut cupboard with bracket feet, three beaded-edge drawers, handmade reproduction with some age, $300; child's ladder-back armchair with old dark worn finish, 22½" high; Chippendale refinished walnut worktable with square legs, top is probably an old replacement, $450.

5 *Shaker Antiques*

The December 1970 issue of the *National Antiques Review* included a lengthy article describing the Brimfield, Massachusetts, Antiques Flea Market of Gordon Reid with a sampling of some of the items offered and their prices. The author of the article was almost overwhelmed by the size of the September 1970 show, which featured "455 exhibitors from all over New England, plus Pennsylvania, Iowa, New Jersey, Michigan, New York, and Delaware with a record attendance this year of over 9000 buyers from all over the country." Among a long list of items that were offered for sale at Brimfield was a "Shaker seed box, original condition, $32."

If time travel is ever a possibility, please reserve two time machine tickets for us to journey back to Brimfield for Gordon Reid's September 1970 antiques festival. We also would need to set aside most of the time machine's cargo hold for the return trip, and several large trucks to carry our purchases home.

Both the Brimfield antiques experience and the prices of Shaker antiques have evolved significantly since 1970. Now the lines for using the portable toilets at Brimfield usually have more than 9000 people in them and Shaker seed boxes are rarely found for less than $1200. There was a relatively small number of "serious" Shaker collectors in 1970 and prices were modest. In the early 1990s there are still a relatively small number of serious Shaker collectors, but prices are no longer modest.

To be a serious collector today takes serious money. In 1970 most people were unaware of the investment potential and scarcity of Shaker-related and Shaker-made items and demonstrated little interest. In the 1990s most Americana collectors are aware of Shaker values but have been taken out of the marketplace quickly because of rapidly escalating prices and the decreasing availability of items.

Shaker Chronology

1736	Ann Lee, the founder of the Shaker movement in America, is born in Manchester, England.
1758	Lee (age 22) joins a religious group in Liverpool.
1762	Lee marries Abraham Standerin.
1774	Lee and a few followers leave England and travel to New York.
1780s	Shakers begin marketing oval boxes.
1784	Lee dies in Niskeyuna (later Watervliet), New York.
1787	Shaker membership reaches 1000.
1790s	Shaker seed industry begins.
1805	Three Shaker brothers travel west to develop communities in Indiana, Kentucky, and Ohio.
1840s	Membership grows to more than 6000 in 19 communities from Maine to Kentucky.
1850s	Rocking chairs made at New Lebanon, New York, are sold to the "world" in large quantities.
1861	New Lebanon becomes Mount Lebanon with a change in the post office.
1871	Shaker magazine begins publication in Canterbury, New Hampshire, and continues under several different names for 29 years until 1900.
1876	Shaker booth at Philadelphia Exposition wins awards and increases chair sales.
1880–1920	"Fancy goods" stores operate in several New England communities and sell to visitors and tourists.
1902	Several Shaker communities indicate that they would accept no new members who were in poor physical condition or more than 50 years of age.

1942	Chair factory building at Mount Lebanon burns.
1947	Mount Lebanon community closes and the remaining members move to Hancock, Massachusetts.
1961	Brother Delmar Wilson, the last male Shaker, dies at Sabbathday Lake, Maine.

Shaker Chairs

The only pieces of Shaker furniture made available to the "world" were a wide variety of chairs and several styles of foot benches or stools. Shaker rocking chairs were made in eight sizes, ranging from a child's chair (0) to the adult version (#7).

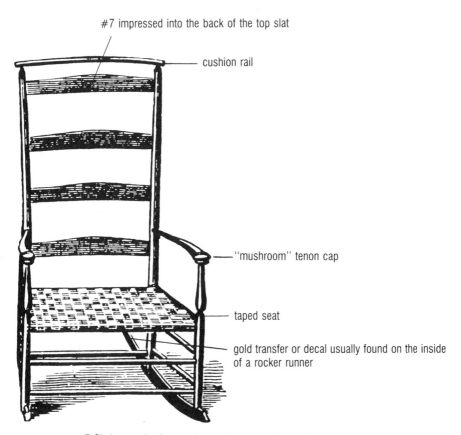

#7 impressed into the back of the top slat

cushion rail

"mushroom" tenon cap

taped seat

gold transfer or decal usually found on the inside of a rocker runner

#7 Shaker production rocking chair comparable to thousands made between 1873 and 1935.

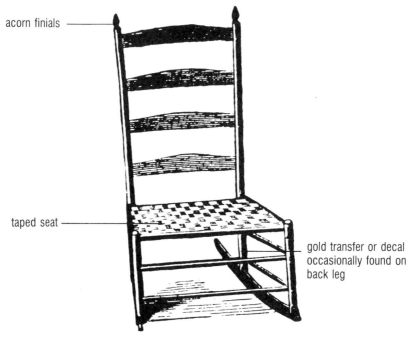

acorn finials

taped seat

gold transfer or decal occasionally found on back leg

#7 Shaker production rocking chair made at Mount Lebanon, New York.

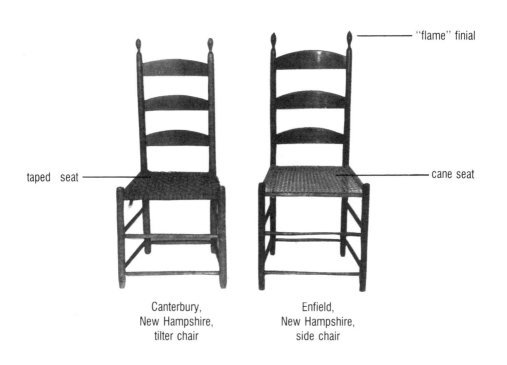

"flame" finial

taped seat

cane seat

Canterbury,
New Hampshire,
tilter chair

Enfield,
New Hampshire,
side chair

Auction Catalogs

Auction catalogs can become an invaluable resource for serious and even casual collectors of Shaker antiques and Americana. The McInnis-Hamel auction catalog is typical of many quality publications from auction houses that are individually researched and prepared for sales.

The catalogs contain professionally taken photographs, detailed information, and the dimensions of each piece to be offered at auction. Collectors who purchase the catalogs normally receive a post-sale listing from the auction house, providing the actual selling price of each piece.

We have selected items from the McInnis-Hamel auction to illustrate a cross section of Shaker pieces that are occasionally made available to collectors (in addition to classic rocking chairs, case pieces such as desks and cupboards, and oval fingered boxes that most people instantly identify with the Shakers).

Results of Shaker Antiques Auctions, 1972–1985

A sampling of results from auctions of Shaker antiques from 1972 to 1985 can provide some insights into today's prices.

Sabbathday Lake, Maine, auction on June 20, 1972

Two-door cupboard with clothespin pulls, 75″ high × 29″ wide × 14″ deep. $700

Henry Greene sewing desk with 12 drawers, Alfred, Maine, butternut and maple, 40½″ tall × 31″ wide × 24″ deep. $3250

Sabbathday Lake one-door cupboard, used in dairy room, 53″ high × 26″ wide × 8½″ deep. $275

Maine auction of Mount Lebanon, New York, Shaker antiques on June 19, 1973

Revolver or swivel chair, 26″ high, chestnut, maple, and pine. $1000

Pine, two-door panel end cupboard with five drawers. $1700

#6 rocking chair with arms. $125

Bed with wooden rollers and traces of old green paint. $625

#7 signed rocking chair with cushion rail. $255

New York City auction of the Lassiter collection on November 13, 1981

Benjamin Young tall case clock. $26,000

Curly maple side chair with tilters. $4180

Pine cupboard, blind front, from Mount Lebanon. $12,500

Pine and maple worktable with two drawers from Mount Lebanon. $5000

Hancock Shaker Village show on October 1–2, 1983

Mount Lebanon #7 rocker with finials and taped back and seat. $1100

Weaver's stool from Maine with yellow wash. $1675

Sabbathday Lake pie safe, red paint and screen front. $2950

Sideboard server from Kentucky with tiger maple panels. $4500

"Two-step" stool with label. $525

Mount Lebanon #7 rocking chair with cushion rail. $1100

#3 rocking chair. $325

#4 straight chair. $750

Child's blanket chest from Sabbathday Lake. $950

#3 Mount Lebanon straight chair. $350

#6 rocking chair with cushion rail. $875

Bentwood rocking chair. $375

#1 child's rocking chair. $1250

#5 rocking chair with finials and a taped back and seat. $850

New Lebanon blanket chest in butternut wood and original paint. $4500

Duxbury, Massachusetts, auction on June 30, 1984

Blue gray blind front cupboard with paneled door, 6′3½″ high. $4950

Canterbury, New Hampshire, side chair, original finish and tilters. $2200

Sabbathday Lake blanket chest, original green paint, lift top with three drawers below. $15,400

Mount Lebanon, New York, revolving chair in black paint, c. 1830. $6600

Chrome yellow three-slat Watervliet rocking chair. $1540

Pittsfield, Massachusetts, auction in summer 1985

Production rocking chairs from Mount Lebanon, New York
#0 without arms. $1375
#1 without arms. $990
#3 without arms (several were sold). $440–$660
#7 without arms. $1045
#7 with arms. $1320

Fitted sewing box with swing handle. $385

New Lebanon, New York, high chair. $11,000

Set of four butternut carriers, rectangular in form with dovetailed sides. $8800

Salmon painted chest, bracket base, four drawers. $3300

Paul McInnis Inc.

On July 28, 1991, the Paul McInnis Inc. Auction Gallery of Hampton Falls, New Hampshire, and internationally respected Shaker dealer Doug Hamel of Concord, New Hampshire, presented an unreserved auction of Shaker antiques.

Information about future auctions can be obtained by contacting:

Paul McInnis Inc.
356 Exeter Road
Hampton Falls, NH 03844
Telephone: (603) 778-8989,
1-800-242-8354
(outside New Hampshire)

The prices which follow, from the McInnis/Hamel Auction, include the 10 percent buyer's premium.

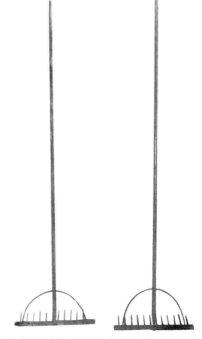

Winnowing sieve, metal perforated winnowing pan with wooden handle, 43½" long, Enfield, Connecticut, $192.50; tin coffeepot with old repairs, 11½" tall, Canterbury, New Hampshire, $275; long-handled dustpan in unusual form with original finish, $385.

Wooden rake in natural finish, 67" high, Enfield, New Hampshire, $55; wooden rake in yellow wash, 67" high, Enfield, New Hampshire, $220.

Swift with original yellow wash, Hancock, Massachusetts, $244.50; chip basket with some damage, Canterbury, New Hampshire, $495; one-drawer worktable of mixed woods and old stain finish, 30" high × 54" wide × 32" deep, attributed to Enfield, New Hampshire, $660.

Swift from Hancock, Massachusetts. **$275**

Sewing carrier with variegated wood top, four fingers, original finish, replaced interior fabric, 9", Mount Lebanon, $605; screw ball clamp with birch base and original finish on green velvet pin cushion, $605; one-piece carved maple apple butter scoop with natural finish, found in Maine, $302.50.

Metal-bound wood chip carrier, appropriate wear, $550; large rectangular cutlery box divided into three sections, $770.

Oblong sewing carrier lined with green satin, $605; swift with original yellow wash, Hancock, Massachusetts, $467.50; herb carrier in original chrome yellow, some damage, three fingers, Canterbury, New Hampshire, $550.

Oval box with original salmon wash, paper label on back "Cochineal" (used in dyes), vertical flaw in wood, 13½" long with five fingers, vertical flaw in wood. **$1210**

Double-handled basket of New England origin.
$247.50

Refinished and retaped #7 Mount Lebanon, New York, rocker with green and cream tape seat. **$935**

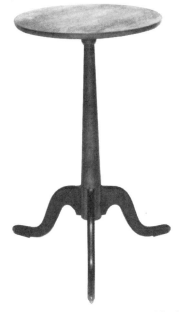

Cherry candlestand, round top with donut, snake leg, shaped metal plate, original finish on base, 25" high × 14¼" diameter, Mount Lebanon, New York. **$11,000**

Armchair rocker with booted leg, old splint seat, and old refinish (repairs), Watervliet, New York. **$1100**

Rocking chair (#3) with arms, dark finish, repaired and replaced seat, Mount Lebanon, New York. **$550**

Three-slat side chair rocker with old refinish and replaced rockers, seat height 15", back posts 38", Sabbathday Lake, Maine. **$385**

Armless Mount Lebanon, New York, rocker (#7) in original finish with tiger maple posts, blue and tan seat. **$825**

Rocking chair (#6) with light natural finish and replaced seat, Mount Lebanon, New York. **$1210**

Canterbury dining chair, pine seat with birch, seat 17½" high. **$880**

Side chair rocker with old finish and rush seat, originally a tilter, seat 15½" high, Enfield, New Hampshire. $770

Canterbury tilter in figured curly and birdseye maple, nice old bubbled finish, early taped seat, one tilter button missing, seat 16½" high, $3300; side chair tilter with cane seat, tilters and seat replaced, old finish, seat 17" high, Enfield, New Hampshire, $2200.

Five-slat Mount Lebanon, New York, armchair in original finish, seat 18½" high, back posts 51½". $3850

Side chair rocker with cane seat and old finish, unusual application of rocker to tilter done by Shakers with additional base support, Enfield, New Hampshire. $2530

Figured maple side chair with rush seat and old refinish, Canterbury, New Hampshire. **$4675**

Refinished side chair with cane seat, tilter, minor repair, seat height 16", back posts 41", Enfield, New Hampshire, **$990;** *youth-size three-slat chair, tilter, old finish, new rush seat, Mount Lebanon, New York,* **$990.**

Side chair tilter with cane seat, Harvard, Massachusetts. **$1650**

Meetinghouse settee with original and original arched metal braces, 10' long, Enfield, New Hampshire. **$11,110**

Early tilter side chair, Mount Lebanon, New York. **$770**

Cupboard over drawers, interior has original mustard color, exterior refinished with some repair, 7' high × 2' deep, Sabbathday Lake, Maine. **$5500**

One-door shop cupboard with original paint and brass knob, 35" tall × 29½" wide × 21½" deep, Hancock, Massachusetts. **$660**

Two-door pine cupboard with original yellow wash, 42" high × 40" wide, Canterbury, New Hampshire. **$1870**

Tall chest with eight drawers, dovetailed case and base, old gray paint over red, c. 1820, 5'9½" high × 43" wide. **$23,100**

Starch table with pine top and maple base, ash stretchers, refinished top, 28" wide × 25" high × 21" deep. **$990**

School double desk from Watervliet, New York, school, obtained from Eldress Anne Case, 26" high × 45½" wide, **$440;** small side chair with original bubbled surface and tilters, cane seat, seat 14½" high, **$1100.**

Pair of mixed wood sewing desks attributed to Elder William Briggs, 40" high at back × 29" wide, Canterbury, New Hampshire. **$14,850 pair**

Refinished writing desk with dovetailed construction, pine with birch tapered and chamfered legs, simple pigeonhole interior, 31" wide × 20" deep × 36" high in back, attributed to Sabbathday Lake, Maine. **$2970**

Birch and pine sewing desk with old refinish, 44" high × 29" wide × 28½" deep, Canterbury, New Hampshire. **$12,100**

Two-drawer blanket chest with thumbnail-molded dovetailed drawer with original classic knobs, modern yellow enamel paint over original red, 40½" high × 37" wide × 19" deep, Enfield, New Hampshire. **$3025**

Five-drawer panelled pine side chest in original finish, dovetailed, lipped drawers, original knobs and escutcheons, minor repair, Watervliet, New York. **$6050**

Four-drawer chest in pine with original worn yellow wash, original diamond keyhole escutcheons, Canterbury, New Hampshire. **$3410**

One-drawer refinished pine blanket chest, 35" high × 35" wide, Enfield, New Hampshire. **$1980**

Footstool in original finish with decal, Mount Lebanon, New York, **$715**; pine drop leaf table with worn surface, old refinish and repairs, 28" high, 5' long, Canterbury, New Hampshire, **$770.**

Cast-iron stove with repair to base made for Enfield, New Hampshire, Shakers in Brandon, Vermont. **$330**

Round hook rug, knitted background with pinwheel center and concentric circles, strong colors. **$1210**

One-drawer stand in original red paint, round tapered legs, 27" high. **$935**

6

*Kitchen and
Hearth Antiques*

This chapter was prepared by Teri and Joe Dziadul and it illustrates items from their personal collection. The Dziaduls have been filling special requests for more than 20 years and offer kitchen and hearth antiques for sale to collectors and dealers. The current list of items for sale may be obtained by sending $1 to the Dziaduls at the following address:

Teri and Joe Dziadul
6 South George Washington Road
Enfield, CT 06082

The bounty that came from the primitive Pilgrim hearth provided the traditional American cooking which we all treasure today. They adapted well to strange native foods which New England yielded. Lobster, quahogs, and cod from the sea; maple syrup from the sugar maple; plus corn, pumpkins, and beans were all reliable sources. Yankee cooks devised ingenious ways to present everything from clams to cranberries.

Five of the New England states face the sea, and the early settlers benefitted through abundant fish and seafood for their own use and export, too. Native products remained popular, but foreign products quickly came. Molasses from the West Indies, tapioca from South America, spices from Indonesia, and tea and ginger from China were in great demand.

Working over open log fires, Pilgrim wives prepared robust dishes for their menfolk. "She that is ignorant in cookery," noted a seventeenth-century proverb, "may love and obey, but she cannot cherish and keep her husband." During their spare moments, wives sat at the spinning wheel making cloth for their families. While the kettle was cooking wild fowl or venison for a stew, it could also cook a sweet pudding in a cloth bag. Cooking in iron kettles, skillets, and Dutch ovens demanded considerable skill as well as constant attention. The real test for the seventeenth-century cook was the brick oven, where wives did their primary baking. Loaves of bread, pies, and cakes were placed strategically inside the brick oven for proper baking time.

When the oven was full, a heavy wooden closely fitted door was shut. The door could be renewed when heavily charred. Many women relied on the sun to tell them when a dish was done. Some kitchens had marks painted on their floors, from which the hours could be read as though on a sundial. Many a cake was timed by the sunbeams creeping across the floorboards.

Pies were eaten at every meal, including breakfast. In winter pies were turned out in vast numbers. An unheated back room held a week's supply. Some housewives baked dozens of pies at a time, froze them in the snow, then thawed and warmed them for each meal in front of the blazing fire on the hearth.

From these early times evolved labor-saving devices that are intriguing reminders of the past and collectibles that are sought after today by serious collectors.

Scotch wrought-iron bread drier, serpentine form supports, leg acts as a stabilizing support, eighteenth century. **$300–$400**

Potato peeler with Hamlinite marking, tin pan and strap handle, ca. 1920, **$35–$45.** *The grit and cement composition sands off the peel.*

Wrought-iron down-hearth revolving broiler for preparing meat or fish over hot coals. **$325–$375**

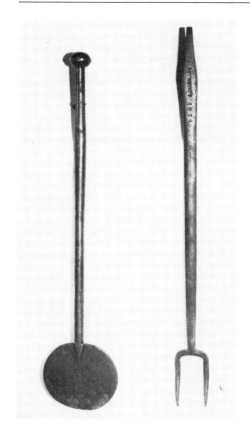

Salamander wrought-iron meat fork, eighteenth century, **$175–$250;** *meat fork, wrought iron, signed "Schmidt," a noted Pennsylvania blacksmith,* **$250–$300.** *The iron disc was put into the fire until red hot. It was then pressed over the tops of bread and pastries for browning without further cooking. Signed and dated pieces always are more valuable.*

Skewer set with cutout heart. **$650–$675**

Treen and iron ladles: treen ladle with perforations for draining, **$300–$350;** *treen ladle with carved hook handle,* **$325–$375;** *iron ladle, signed "J. Schmidt" and dated 1854, made by noted Pennsylvania blacksmith,* **$275–$325.**

Wrought-iron potato rake, rare. **$250–$275.** *This was used to scoop potatoes out of hot coals in an open hearth.*

Ice cream scoops: Indestructo Benedict Deluxe,
$75–$85; *Zeroll of Maumee, Ohio, aluminum model, handle contains a self-defrosting liquid, aluminum, ca. 1934,* **$25–$30;**
Medco of New York City, ca. 1939, **$75–$85.**

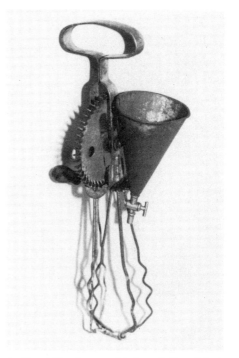

Le Tourbillon beater with funnel, funnel hooks on side of beater to pour oil for making mayonnaise, shut-off valve on funnel to regulate flow of oil. **$225–$275**

Whippers and beaters: Quarter beater,
$65–$75; *LeRoides beater,* **$85–$95;** *spiral whipper,* **$55–$65.**

Beater jars: Holt's Improved, Holt-Lyon, Tarrytown, New York, **$140–$150;** *Presto Churn,* **$125–$135.**

Unmarked one-quart butter churn. **$145–$175**

Oversized tin pastry cutter and crimper with brass ferrule, 18 inches long, punched hearts around border of wheel, **$400–$500.** *This may have been hung in a bakery or given as a tenth wedding anniversary gift.*

Baldwin cast-iron apple peeler, ca. 1870. **$135–$150**

Cast-iron apple peeler with an unusual push off, apparently made by F. W. Hudson. **$150–$175**

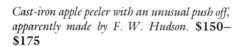

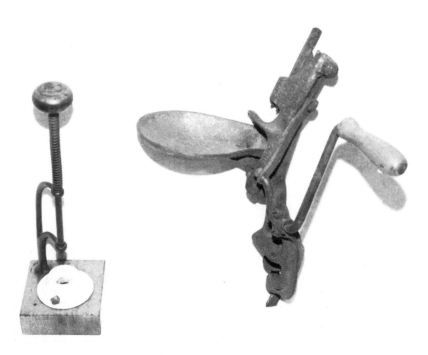

Cherry stoners: wood, iron, and porcelain peeler with push knob, iron shaft with spring action stones one cherry at a time, scarce version, **$100–$150;** *cast-iron peeler with screw-on clamp, Mount Joy, Pennsylvania, ca. 1900,* **$50–$65.**

Lathe-type cast-iron apple peeler mounted on wooden base made prior to the Civil War by D. H. Whittemore. **$200–$225**

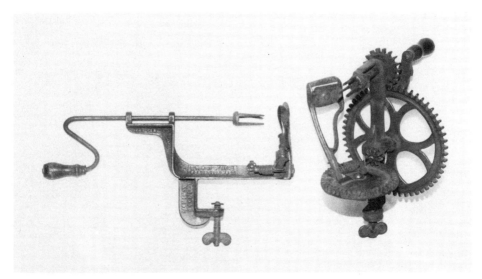

Cast-iron apple peelers: embossed "D. H. Whittemore, Worcester, Mass., Pat. Ext. Jan 18, 1871," **$150–$175;** *#72, produced by Reading Hardware Co., scarce version with larger drive wheel,* **$150–$175.**

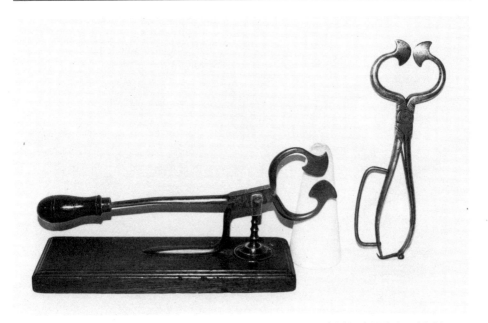

Sugar cutters: mounted on board to cut up large pieces of cone sugar, **$350–$375;** *hand-held sugar nippers used at the table to cut cone sugar,* **$225–$250.** *Sugar cutters were used to cut cone sugar into small pieces. The small pieces then were pulverized for kitchen use.*

Shaker stove pipe shelf, **$175–$200.** *This was a tin collar fitted around the stove pipe to keep food warm.*

Cyclone cast-iron egg beater with perforated flanges, ca. 1901, **$125–$150;** *sugar cutter,* **$225–$250.**

Dovetailed covered copper pot with iron handles, made in New York, **$350–$375;** *Clark iron porringer, marked "Bellevue" on tab,* **$125–$175.**

E Z Corn Popper, tin with wooden handle. **$55–$75**

115

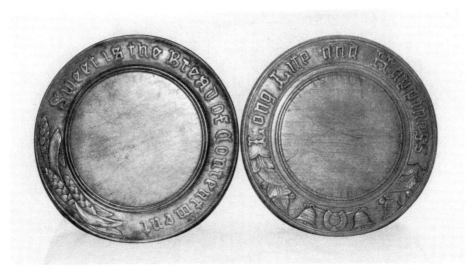

Wooden bread boards with very unusual carved borders, which increase value substantially: "Sweet is the Bread of Contentment," $275–$350; "Long Life and Happiness" wedding board, $300–$375.

Wooden bread boards: "The Staff of Life," $150–$200; "Cut and Come Again," $250–$300.

Maple bread board, "Bread" carved on border, $55–$75; knife with steel blade, handle with "Bread" carved on cartouche, $65–$85.

Wood plate rack, $250–$275; Wedgwood plates, $55–$65 each.

Plate rack, $275–$300; Wedgwood plates, $45–$55 each.

Treen nutmeg grater, ca. 1825, $500–$600. Iron crank propeller-type handle grates several nutmegs at one time.

Treen teapot tile, ca. 1890, **$75–$95**; *pewter teapot with rose finial,* **$175–$200.**

Tin nutmeg graters: grater with round hinged cover for nutmeg storage, an unusual form, **$75–$85**; *pie-shaped grater with swivel action to grate nutmeg, marked "Lynn, Mass. Patented Oct. 13 1857,"* **$650–$750**; *tin nutmeg grater, marked "pat. by W. Bradley, Lynn, Mass. Pat. Jan. 29, 1867,"* **$375–$425.**

Wall-hung spice chest, eight-drawer unit, wood knobs, pewter scroll labels on drawers. **$350–$400**

Wood-grained chest, painted surface resembles birdseye and tiger maple graining. **$475–$575**

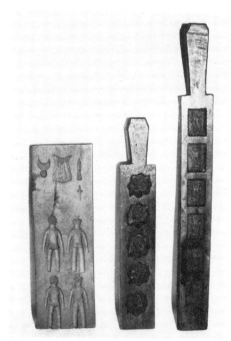

Confectioner's mold and cookie board molds: treen mold to form decorations for pastries, **$300–$350;** *treen molds to impress designs on cookie dough,* **$45–$55.**

St. Nicholas wallbox with original paint, hinged lid, and folk art carving. **$1200–$1500**

Wallbox, painted red, with folk art carving. **$500–$550**

Spice boxes: tin, painted red with gold stencil, $125–$175; tin, with nutmeg grated and stenciled cover, $175–$200; three-tier spice tower, ca. 1820, $325–$375.

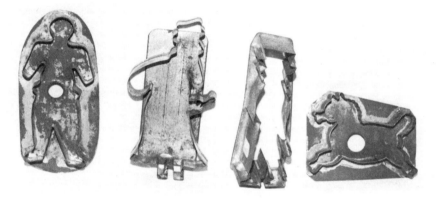

Tin cookie cutters: man, $125–$150; Father Christmas with sack, $150–$200; Uncle Sam, $150–$200; horse, $125–$150.

Butter stamps: deeply carved swirling swastika, $375–$450; cow with gate and branch, intricate border, $275–$325; creel of fish, a very rare subject, $500–$600.

Miniature portrait on ivory of Oliver Hazard Perry. $1650 at Copake auction

Early twentieth-century dry sink with zinc-lined well. $475–$575

Painted pine woodbox, c. 1900. **$650–$800**

Three splint country baskets, early twentieth century. **$125–$175** *each*

Elaborately decorated jug signed "C. & E. Norton, Bennington, Vt.," nineteenth century. **$2000–$3000**

Blind-front pine cupboard with bracket base, c. 1860. **$1800–$2000**

Painted Pennsylvania dry sink, c. 1860. **$1500–$2000**

Nineteenth-century portrait attributed to Ammi Philips. $2850 at Copake auction.

Country blind-front corner cupboard, c. 1840. $1500–$1800

Two-gallon stenciled crock. $95–$115

Maple and pine kitchen cabinet, c. 1920. $600–$700

Painted pie cupboard, c. 1880. $895 at Country Village

Factory-made dome-top trunk, c. early 1900s. $100–$150

Painted pine pie cupboard, c. mid-nineteenth century. $700–$800

Painted pine pie cupboard, c. 1870. $600–$800

Dry sink in apple green and mustard paint, late nineteenth century. **$1750** *at Country Village*

Butter stamps: heart, leaves, and double border, **$350–$400;** *vigilant cow, grass, and branch,* **$350–$400;** *miniature rooster,* **$375–$450.**

Butter stamps: pine lollypop version with geometric print, New England, **$300–$375;** *game bird— an unusual subject,* **$300–$375.**

Butter molds and stamp: rooster butter mold, scarce subject, **$475–$525;** *quail butter stamp, rare,* **$450–$475;** *pelican butter mold, very scarce subject,* **$500–$550.**

Confection mold used for making cake decorations, $200–$275; treen lathe-turned muffineer in fine condition, $275–$300.

Butter stamps: deeply carved pineapple, $150–$200; skillful floral carving with extreme depth, $145–$175; double acorns and oak leaves, deep carving, $145–$175.

Tin toaster, ca. 1910, $20–$30; tin biscuit cutter, an advertising piece by Rumford, $18–$25. The toaster was placed over an open flame, and the bread had to be turned by hand.

Blown blue Christmas light, $95–$125; blue skater's lantern, $300–$350; blue hobnail light with tin screw-on bottom, $125–$175.

Treenware: funnel, $85–$125; noggin, $125–$200; covered sugar bowl with bail handle, $450–$500.

Make-do's: goblet, champagne flute with tin stem repair, goblet with tin stem and base replacement, $125–$175 each.

*Ice cream penny licks: tuppeny lick, **$55–$75**; penny lick, **$55–$75**; pressed glass tuppeny lick with polished pontil, **$75–$85**. These glasses were used by ice cream vendors when ice cream was sold by penny or two-penny licks. Poor sanitation in washing after use and epidemic tuberculosis caused licks to fall from favor.*

*Miniature treen pieces: castor set, **$150–$175**; goblet with ring, **$75–$85**; open salt, **$55–$65**; jug with iron handle, **$40–$45**; food chopper with bone handle, **$200–$250**.*

Copper ale boot and tin ale slipper, both ca. 1800. Copper boot, **$550–$650;** *tin slipper,* **$400–$450.** *Home-brewed ale was warmed in these pieces by thrusting them into coals in an open hearth.*

Tin wall candle sconce with crimped edge. **$325–$350**

Round tin candle mold with hanging ring, unusual form, fine condition. **$1000–$1200**

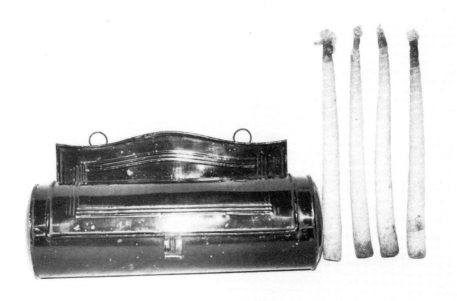

Tin candlebox with original finish, $275–$350; *old tallow candles, ca. eighteenth century,* $75–$100 **each.**

Large trug basket with gilt painting on the inside, $275–$300. *Most trug baskets are rectangular; this one is round and probably was used as a large gathering basket.*

Higgins basket with original maker's stamp on bottom, $425–$475. *Prices for Higgins baskets have increased dramatically in recent years.*

Splint utility basket in excellent condition. $275–$300

Splint utility basket with fine splint weaving. $275–$300

Strawberry baskets with coarsely woven splint construction. $75–$85 each

Apple gathering hip basket with leather strap tied to handles and hung over the shoulder, $325–$375; splint gathering basket in unusual size, $125–$175.

Swing handle basket in large market basket size, with exceptional woven workmanship. **$425–$475**

Picnic basket with wooden cover and handles and sturdy splint construction. **$125–$150**

Woven poplar Shaker bonnet from Enfield community, fine condition. **$250–$300**

Pine oval-staved carrier with copper bands and cutout heart handles. **$500–$575**

Stone fruit: pear, banana, figs, peach, lemon, plum, almond, and walnuts. **$125–$175 each**

Sled in fine condition with blue paint, lathe-turned ornamentation on each side, and painted flowers and striping. **$375–$450**

Sled with red paint, inset iron under the runners, and painted flowers and striping. **$350–$400**

Doris Stauble arrangement with melons and other fruit in old painted blue bowl, with old millinery material as filler between pieces. **$325–$375**

Windsor stool with original finish. **$250–$275**

Original contemporary watercolor painting by Tasha Tudor that appears in the book All for Love *(New York: Putnam Publishing Group, 1984) on page 39.* **$4000–$4500**

Milliner's head with calf-skin leather cap on original working milliner's model, rare with leather covering. **$1200–$1400**

Wooden Santa mold to make papier-mâché containers. **$350–$400**

Shaker kitchen by Gus Schwertefeger, chairs marked with "S." Chairs, $150–$175; room, $1200. A close friend of the Shakers, he made a limited number of rooms and accurately scaled miniature pieces with taped seats when he was in his 80s. Now deceased, his pieces are eagerly sought.

Doris Stauble arrangement with old millinery materials in old containers, $200–$250. Arrangements by this contemporary folk artist are very popular.

Covered four-gallon crock signed "F. H. Cowden, Harrisburg," with cobalt blue design, more desirable with original cover. $400–$500

Stoneware blind pig with cobalt blue decoration that held beer or hard cider, spigot inserted in opening of flat end. **$700–$800**

Ovoid stoneware jug with "Boston" impressed on banner, ocher color. **$400–$450**

Papier-mâché owls: double-sided owl with glass eyes and metal prong at base for mounting on roof, marked "Boules Swisher, Decatur, Illinois," **$90–$100**; papier-mâché owl with glass eyes, **$90–$100**.

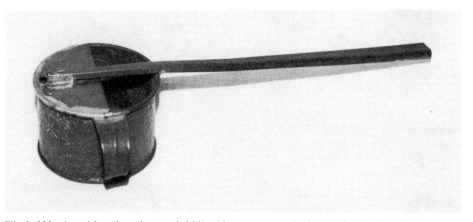

Tin bubble pipe with embossed cup to hold liquid, a rare example, **$125–$175**. Liquid is drawn up inner stem when child blows through the pipe.

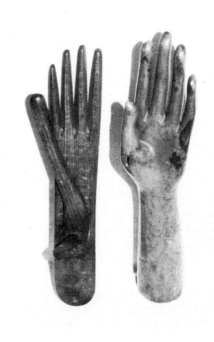

Small butter churns: tin with original wooden dasher, body 13 inches high, **$275–$300;** *stoneware churn signed "Swan & States, Stonington," an early potter, ca. 1823–1835,* **$450–$500.** *Small churns command higher prices.*

Treen glove forms: left one has moveable thumb secured by a wood screw; right has hinged thumb, carved nails on fingers give this piece a folk art feel, **$225–$275 each.** *Glove forms were secured to a table.*

7 *Decorated Stoneware*

Decorated American stoneware is primarily a product of the nineteenth century. In the late 1700s there were a few stoneware potteries operating in urban areas (New York, Boston) and almost none in rural settings. The smaller rural potteries in the late eighteenth century produced redware rather than stoneware crocks and jugs. Redware was turned out in huge quantities from the mid-1600s until almost 1900 in some rural areas.

The clays used in the manufacture of redware pottery could be found easily with a shovel in most areas of Pennsylvania. The redware was fragile, difficult to transport any distance, and extremely porous. It was also sealed with a colorless glaze that contained a great deal of lead.

Redware potters rarely signed or marked their pieces with a stamp, which makes any attempt at dating or identifying where or when a piece of redware pottery was made an extremely difficult proposition.

After 1800 the number of stoneware potteries in the eastern United States gradually increased from a few to hundreds by the middle of the century. Stoneware products were in demand with nineteenth-century consumers because they were fired in kilns to more than 2100 degrees Fahrenheit and were water tight. Stoneware also was much more durable than redware, easily cleaned, and could take extremes of heat and cold with no problems. Unlike the lead glaze on redware that slowly and silently killed some unsuspecting consumers over time, stoneware potters used a salt glaze that presented no health problems.

Stoneware was the dominant form of household storage for food and drink until the turn of this century, when inexpensive mass-produced glass jars and bottles and home refrigeration took away most of the business and closed the potteries.

Collecting Nineteenth-Century Stoneware

Unlike art pottery from the first half of the twentieth century, that was designed to be collected and displayed on an oak table from Sears or given to Aunt Hilda and Uncle Wilbur as an anniversary gift, decorated American stoneware was totally utilitarian. It was produced to hold water or spirits in jugs ranging up to five gallons or garden produce in large crocks.

Almost all pieces of stoneware that potential buyers have an opportunity to inspect in private collections, shops, or at auctions are flawed to varying degrees. It is almost a given that every piece of stoneware is less than perfect. The flaws are to be expected because stoneware was a hands-on product that also was subject to numerous variables that were impossible to control once it was placed in the kiln for the firing process. Among the many flaws may be cracks, "fried" cobalt, flaking glaze, chips, burns or brown spots, or "salt tears."

There are several varieties of cracks that may appear on a piece of stoneware that can affect its desirability and value. A "drying line" is usually a harmless crack in the clay that happened while the piece was being dried prior to being placed in the kiln. Drying lines are covered by the salt-glazing process in the kiln and are not considered serious. A hairline crack by definition does not extend through the body of the piece of stoneware. It is a thin surface crack. A crack that goes through usually has to be repaired or undergo a restoration process. The problem comes into play when the hairline crack is being evaluated. Sometimes the hairline evolves into a through crack over time.

If the kiln became too hot during the firing process and there was too much water in the cobalt slip (a mixture of cobalt oxide and liquid clay), the cobalt decoration often bubbled or burned away. Since most collectors are primarily interested in decoration, a cobalt bird on a jug that has bubbled over or fried loses value. Other flaws in the decoration process sometimes occurred when the heat generated in the kiln turned the normally blue cobalt black or blurred the decoration and caused it to run or blur.

Collectors are especially concerned about flaking glaze because it cannot be controlled. In a sense flaking is like a cancer that alternates between periods of aggressiveness and periods of remission.

Stoneware was inexpensive and readily available to most Americans after 1840. It was used daily, and consequently many pieces were chipped on their bases, pouring spouts, or rims. Most pieces of decorated stoneware that have great value and chipped areas are usually professionally restored. Canning jars with chips priced at $100 normally are enjoyed without the necessity of professional assistance.

If a piece of stoneware was too close to the fire in the kiln, a brown spot or kiln burn usually resulted. It is not uncommon to find a piece of stoneware that has the glaze burned off down to the surface on a section of the crock or jug.

A salt tear gives the impression that someone has expectorated on the side of the piece. Salt tears are greenish bubbles created when the kiln cooled off too quickly, combined with an overabundance of salt in the kiln.

Decoration

Four major techniques were used to decorate nineteenth-century American stoneware. These included incising, brushing, slip-cupping or slip-trailing, and stenciling.

Incising

Incising was a process popular among potters from the late eighteenth century through the first quarter of the nineteenth century. The decorator used a metal tool or a sharp piece of wire to scratch a flower, bird, ship, or capacity mark into the surface of the stoneware. Incised stoneware is difficult to find, as relatively few pieces have survived and elaborately decorated pieces command serious dollars. Even though only a small minority of the nation's stoneware collectors actively seek incised examples, they typically are forced to pay much higher prices than individuals who seek out the best in jugs, crocks, and churns decorated using a brush or slip-cup.

Slip-cupping or Trailing

Slip-cupping or slip-trailing involved pouring a thin line of cobalt slip

from a "cup" in a process similar to decorating a cake. The slip-cupping left a raised line of cobalt decoration on the surface of the stoneware. This technique was used from the late 1830s through the 1880s, with some of the best examples being produced in the 1850s and 1860s.

Brushing

Brushed decoration was achieved by dipping a brush in cobalt slip and painting the surface of the stoneware. Designs ranged from simple swirls and capacity marks to scenes of circus acrobats, battleships, or exotic animals like zebras and elephants. The brush was the most commonly used tool to decorate stoneware between 1850 and the 1880s.

Stenciling

Stenciling was the last decorating technique used on stoneware. The decade of the 1880s saw a gradual change at most potteries that eventually led to the mechanization of stoneware production and the demise of local potteries that made pieces on a potter's wheel. It

Contemporary crock from the Bon Aqua, Tennessee, pottery with classic slip-trailed bird and ground cover.

Miniature jug with incised message from Ginder's Cash Store, Altoona, Pa. The Albany slip jug dates from 1890–1900.

Contemporary piece of stoneware with slip-trailed or slip-cupped swan, from the pottery of Jerry Beaumont.

Contemporary churn entirely covered with slip-trailed scene of a village, from the Beaumont Pottery.

Stenciled crock, molded rather than hand thrown, Bristol glaze, c. early 1900s.

had become too expensive to have an individual potter produce a piece and to employ a decorator to hastily brush on a splash of cobalt. Molded stoneware was decorated with a stencil rather than a brush or slip-cup. Stoneware with stenciled decoration dates from the early 1880s to the 1920s, at which point most stoneware potteries in the United States went out of business.

Restoration and Repair

One of the first pieces of stoneware we purchased was a two-gallon crock with a major through crack on one side. At some point a wire had been securely wrapped around the crock and tightened to the point that the crack was virtually invisible and the piece was almost watertight. The wire was a legitimate attempt at repairing a piece that still was useful. If the crock was restored rather than repaired, the wire would be taken away and a lengthy process of sealing the crack and making it disappear would begin.

Most collectors would not spend twice the value of the crock to have it professionally restored. They would live with the repair, as we have for 25 years, and enjoy the crock as is.

A four-gallon crock with a cobalt elephant racing past several palm trees that has a major rim chip and a through crack from top to bottom presents a different problem. It will have its value enhanced considerably by being professionally restored. To attempt to repair the rim chip and crack could only diminish its value and make the inevitable restoration even more complex and expensive.

When a piece is restored, it is returned, as close as possible, to its original condition. The restoration involves removing flaws (cracks, chips) that it picked up in daily use over time *after* it was removed from the kiln. Brown spots and other kiln-related flaws are part of its original condition and are not addressed by the restoration.

A collector purchasing a major piece of stoneware should expect to be told about any restoration that has taken place. The receipt or bill of sale should point out in detail exactly what has been done.

"We Get Letters"

Over the years we have received many calls and letters from collectors who have uncovered a piece of Americana about which they have questions. We thought that the following episode was worth sharing. David Beier's "find" sounded reasonably legitimate over the telephone. The piece of stoneware was impressed with a nineteenth-century mark, it turned up at a rural auction consisting primarily of household goods, and sold for a small fraction of its potential worth. (The following article was written for this edition at our request by David W. Beier.)

Close-up photograph of three-gallon stoneware jug from the late nineteenth century, signed "F. Woodworth, Burlington, Vt.," with contemporary decoration of Indian warrior, purchased for $50 at 1991 auction.

On Thursday October 10, 1991, I attended a sale at a small auction barn in upstate New York. A friend, who had to be at work, asked me to be there to bid on an old piano for him. During the auction preview I spotted several jugs and crocks which appeared to be in excellent condition. One piece of particular interest to me was a three-gallon jug marked "F. Woodworth, Burlington, Vt." It was decorated with a full-figure Indian in cobalt slip. I had never seen anything like it. Most of the stoneware in my collection was produced in nearby Bennington, Vermont.

The jug came up for bid, starting at $5. It reached $50 and was mine. The piano went too high.

On Friday I was in Bennington and decided to stop at a bookstore. At this point I was most interested in researching the pottery mark on the jug. I found a book, Country Stoneware, *by Don and Carol Raycraft. In the beginning of the book there are explanations of terms and decorations and it indicated that human figures were especially rare. Listed in the front of the book was Mr. and Mrs. Raycraft's address. I called information and spoke with Mr. Raycraft at home on Saturday morning. I described the details of the jug to Mr. Raycraft. He sounded excited and proceeded to tell me that he felt the value of the piece was at the very least $3000 to $5000 if it was old. I was in shock. He*

Collectors should be wary of undecorated nineteenth-century stoneware with a potter's mark having its value enhanced significantly with the addition of late-twentieth-century painted birds, human figures, or animals.

also told me of a gentleman who had a large collection of decorated stoneware who lived in the Bennington vicinity, and should I have an interest in selling it, I should certainly give him an opportunity to purchase it. He also told me about a stoneware auction held in Bennington sometime in October each year. I sent photos of the jug to Mr. Raycraft and the private collector he suggested.

I decided the jug was too valuable to have in my home. I called the collector at his home only to discover he was on vacation. I was told he would be returning home before the weekend for, coincidentally, the stoneware auction in Bennington. I felt pressured as to which way I should turn in selling. If the collector wasn't interested, I might miss out on the auction. I called the hotel where the auction was to be held and talked to someone in the business office who gave me the name and number of the man who ran the auction.

I called him and described the jug. He informed me he had recently seen a similar Indian-decorated piece sell for $14,000. I asked him if he would accept this piece into his auction and he agreed. On Thursday, October 17, I received a telephone call from the collector. He advised me that in order to get the highest possible price, the auction was probably my best bet. I asked him if he had received the photo I had sent. At that point he had not gone through his accumulated mail. That evening he called me back with the bad news. He felt I had purchased a fake. I then called the auction sponsor, who made arrangements to meet with me on Friday night to confirm or deny the collector's suspicions.

On Friday evening, the stoneware jug with the cobalt Indian was verified to be nothing more than an old jug with a newly painted decoration.

Pottery-Related Terms

There are some basic terms that relate to collecting pottery that should be a part of every collector's working vocabulary. Out of a potential glossary of hundreds of words, we have selected a dozen. Keep in mind that the educational process is a slow one and this is just a small first step.

China

Now almost a generic term for crockery tableware made from clays of varying quality, this term originally was used to describe high-quality porcelain tableware imported from the Orient in the eighteenth and nineteenth centuries.

Glaze

A shiny, glasslike coating that seals pottery to make it watertight, glaze also can bring out the natural color of the clay. Rock salt was used to add a glaze and "orange peel" appearance to the surface of stoneware after the set was thrown into the kiln at the height of the firing process and quickly vaporized over the contents.

Porcelain

A high-quality hard-paste china comprised of kaolin clay and feldspar, porcelain has been made in the Orient for almost 1500 years.

Hard Paste

This is a mixture of kaolin clay and petuntse (a clay with feldspar) fired at high temperature and used to make porcelain.

Soft Paste

This paste is made from a combination of more common clays and fired at a lower temperature than hard paste. Soft paste requires that the glaze be watertight, and usually is decorated because the the combination of soft-paste clays easily absorbs the decoration.

Redware

The first form of pottery produced in North America was redware. The clay was fired at relatively low temperature (1400°F) and glazed with lead. The clay used often was found at surface level. Redware pottery clays were porous and most of the pieces were glazed on the inside to keep the liquid contents from seeping through the clay.

Sgraffito

Redware pottery that has been coated in slip and then had decorations scratched or incised through the slip and into the pottery's surface is known as sgraffito. Sgraffito-decorated redware was more ornamental than functional. In recent years more sgraffito-decorated redware has come out of Portugal, Mexico, and Spain than Pennsylvania.

Slipware

Redware pottery that has been decorated with a creamy substance made of clay called "slip" is known as slipware. The slip was poured from a cup or applied with a simple tubelike utensil. Most American slipware was made in Pennsylvania. Words, short phrases, or simple designs were added to the redware for decoration or presentation.

Albany Slip

This dark brown slip made from Hudson River clays was used most often to line the inside of stoneware jugs, churns, crocks, and jars. This slip also was used as an exterior slip on late nineteenth-century to early twentieth-century stoneware that was generally molded rather than thrown on a potter's wheel.

Rockingham

A mottled, glazed surface that was popular on utilitarian pottery from the 1820s until 1900, Rockingham glaze was used on Toby jugs, pitchers, mixing bowls, cake pans, and other pieces. Some molded pieces came from Bennington, Vermont, and other much more numerous, unmarked examples were produced in potteries in Illinois, Ohio, and Massachusetts.

Stoneware

Utilitarian pottery made from non-porous (watertight) clays fired at high temperatures (2300°F) was known as stoneware. The glaze is applied by adding rock salt to the kiln. American stoneware is primarily a product of the nineteenth century.

Yellowware

Another form of molded utilitarian stoneware made in huge quantities in the United States and England during the nineteenth and twentieth centuries, yellowware is covered with a clear or colorless glaze which enhances the natural color of the clay.

The Waasdorp Collection

Vicki and Bruce Waasdorp are antiques dealers who specialize in nineteenth-century Americana and accessories in original condition. They have a special interest in decorated stoneware pottery and publish a semi-annual illustrated price list of stoneware that they have for sale.

Much of their business is conducted by mail with novice and advanced collectors and antiques dealers from throughout the United States. The stoneware photographs that follow are from the Waasdorp collection. Information may be secured by contacting:

Vicki and Bruce Waasdorp
10931 Main Street
Clarence, NY 14031
Telephone: (716) 759-2361

Cream pot signed "J. and E. Norton, Bennington, Vt." with reclining spotted deer decoration. **$3500 plus**

Edmonds & Company four-gallon crock with rare deer decoration. **$4500 plus**

Rare unsigned stoneware funnel. **$100–$175**

Two-gallon crock signed "W. H. Farrar, Geddes, N.Y." with bird and flower decoration. **$1150–$1450**

Unsigned two-gallon bird crock. **$275–$375**

Fort Edward, New York, jug with large bird and plume decoration. **$650–$850**

Unsigned batter pail with rare bird decoration. $950–$1150

Two-gallon jug signed "Whites, Utica, N.Y." *with peacock on a stump decoration.* $1200 plus

Three-gallon jar signed "J. & E. Norton, Bennington, Vt." with rare peacock on a stump. $1400 plus

Two-gallon jug signed "W. Roberts, Binghamton, N.Y." with bird decoration. $600–$800

Selection of unsigned stoneware mugs attributed to the White's Utica factory. **$75 plus each**

Unsigned one-gallon batter jug with floral decoration. **$450–$550**

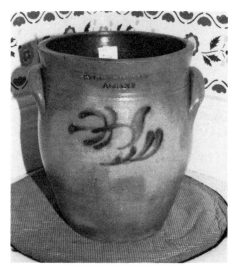

Early ovoid jar with simple flower decoration, New York State. **$250–$400**

Rare milk pan with cobalt decoration, signed "S. Perry, West Troy" (N.Y.). **$450–$650**

One-and-one-half-gallon crock signed "J. Norton and Co., Bennington, Vt." with cobalt bird decoration. **$600 plus**

Stenciled advertising jug with unusual blued top. **$275–$375**

Crock signed "John Burger, Rochester" with detailed daisy. **$400–$600**

One-gallon preserve jar signed "Cortland" with brushed floral decoration. **$375–$475**

Three-gallon churn signed "E. & L. P. Norton, Bennington, Vt." with very rare well-detailed basket of flowers. **$4000 plus**

Six-gallon churn signed "T. Harrington, Lyons" (N.Y.) with brushed flowers. **$450–$550**

"Chicken pecking corn" crock signed "J. Norton & Co., Bennington, Vt." **$1000 plus**

Four-gallon crock signed "A. K. Ballard, Burlington, Vt." with grapes. **$700–$900**

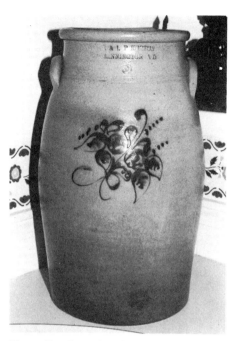

Three-gallon jug signed "J. & E. Norton, Bennington, Vt." with detailed basket of flowers decoration. **$1200–$1600**

Five-gallon churn signed "E. and L. P. Norton, Bennington, Vt." with dotted leaf spray. **$550–$650**

Floral decorated ovoid crock signed "Lyons," New York. **$275–$375**

Elaborate bird and plume on a store-marked jug. **$750–$950**

Three-gallon churn signed "E. and L. P. Norton, Bennington, Vt." with bird on plume decoration. $750–$850

Three-gallon jug signed "Stezenmeyer and Goetzman, Rochester, N.Y.," with detailed dotted flower and rare maker's mark. $1400–$1600

Ovoid jar with brushed floral decoration signed "Clark, Athens, NY." $350–$450

Early jar signed "C. Boynton & Co., Troy" with Roman-numeral-like decoration. $650–$750

Four-gallon crock signed "Whites, Utica" with detailed running bird. **$650–$850**

Flower-decorated jug signed "Burger, Rochester, NY." **$400–$600**

Two 2-gallon crocks signed "Burger, Rochester, NY" with detailed flower decorations. **$300–$600 each**

Early, almost ball-shaped ovoid jug signed "Jacob Caire & Co., Po'keepsie" with simple decoration. **$300 plus**

One-gallon "pine tree" jug signed "Whites, Utica, NY." **$150–$250**

One-gallon jug signed "M. Woodruff, Cortland" with "pine tree" decoration. **$150–$250**

One-gallon ovoid preserve jar signed "Lyons." **$250–$375**

Ovoid jug signed "T. Harrington, Lyons" with large cobalt flower. **$375–$475**

Two-gallon jug with detailed floral decoration and store mark. **$400–$600**

Cream pot signed "Mantell, Penn Yan" (N.Y.) with large basket of flowers. **$875–$975**

Four-gallon crock signed "J. Burger Jr., Rochester, N.Y." with double flower. **$650–$750**

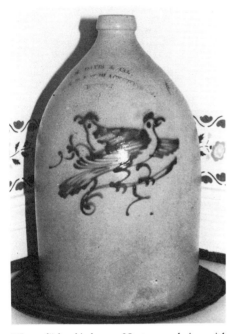

"Crossed" lovebirds on a Norton made jug with a store or vendor's mark. **$950–$1150**

Four-gallon jug signed "N.A. White and Son, Utica, N.Y." with large paddle-tail bird decoration, damage to the spout. **$500–$600 with damage**

Unsigned crock with huge "chicken pecking corn" and through crack. **$575–$775 without crack**

One-gallon bird jug. **$500–$700**

Two-gallon bird-decorated jug signed "Hart's" (Fulton, N.Y.). **$375–$475**

Two-gallon jug with simple brushed design signed "Lyons" (N.Y.). **$150–$250**

Two-gallon jug signed "N. A. White and Son, Utica, N.Y." **$275–$375**

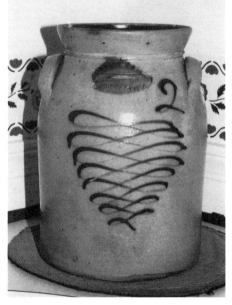

Two-gallon preserve jar with tornado design. **$250–$350**

Two-gallon bird-decorated crock signed "E. W. Hale, Boston." **$350–$450**

Three-gallon crock signed "J. Burger Jr., Rochester, N.Y." with floral decoration. **$250–$350**

Unsigned one-gallon milk pitcher, probably from New York State. **$450–$550**

One-gallon milk pitcher signed "John Burger, Rochester." **$900 plus**

Three-gallon cream pot signed "T. Harrington, Lyons" (N.Y.) with double flower. **$450–$650**

Three-gallon crock signed "F. Norton, Worcester, Mass." with parrot decoration. **$450–$550**

Four-gallon preserve jar with brushed floral decoration. **$450–$650**

Cream pot with bird decoration signed "Norton, Bennington, Vt." **$600–$700**

Three-gallon crock signed "De Weston, Ellenville, N.Y." with detailed bird. **$350–$450**

Three-gallon crock signed "John Burger, Rochester" with detailed double floral decoration. **$750 plus**

Two-gallon preserve jar signed "Lyons" (N.Y.) with brushed floral decoration. **$450–$650**

8 *Graniteware*

Graniteware, also known as enamelware, agateware, porcelainware, glazedware, or speckleware, was a popular kitchenware from its first American manufacture in the 1860s to 1930, when the marketing of aluminum products caused its rapid decline in demand.

European countries were producing graniteware as early as 1838. In the 1860s mass production in the United States was initiated almost simultaneously by three companies: Vollrath of Sheboygan, Wisconsin, LaLance and Grosjean of Woodhaven, New York, and the St. Louis Stamping Company of St. Louis, Missouri.

Graniteware is manufactured by putting a double- or triple-coated enamel surface over iron or steel base metals. Popular colors of graniteware include blue, cobalt blue, and gray. More unusual colors are green, brown, and copper red. Because of the great number of manufacturers, graniteware colors and decorations vary. Solid or shaded colors and the introduction of white through mottling, marbling, and speckling are examples of variations. White graniteware trimmed in cobalt blue, red, or black has been growing in popularity among many collectors in recent years.

Graniteware includes a wide range of items, from pots and pans to toiletry items. Serious collectors search for rare examples such as pewter-trimmed pieces, butter churns, stoves, sinks, and dustpans. Some items are considered rare because of their color or limited quantities. For example, butter churns, declared unsafe for sanitary reasons by the federal government, were produced for only a short time.

Some graniteware collectors also search for advertising that features graniteware. Paper items available include magazine ads, premium cards, catalogs, cookbooks, instruction booklets, and cardboard signs. Trade cards are especially desirable.

Advertising items made of graniteware include signs, cups, ashtrays, serving trays, and salesman's samples. Other area of collectibles feature items made of graniteware and marked with identifying names or letters. Examples are railroad dishes bearing the initials of a particular company such as UPRR (Union Pacific Railroad), and military items.

Children's pieces and miniatures always have been avidly sought by graniteware and toy collectors. They command even higher prices in today's market. Miniatures often were used as toys, and children's pieces such as cups and plates were placed on the table along with adult-size tableware.

Since graniteware is still being produced, it is important to distinguish between old and new. Check the gauge of the base metal. Generally, the heavier the steel or cast iron, the older the piece will be. Pieces with cast-iron handles date from 1870 to 1890; those with wooden handles are from 1900 to 1910. When searching for old graniteware, also look for seams, wooden knobs, and tin lids.

Prices of individual pieces of graniteware are a function of condition, type of molding (pattern of swirls), size of the item, color, and degree of rarity. For example, a one-cup gray coffeepot in mint condition may be offered for $175 to $230. An example in comparable condition and color but several sizes larger may sell for only $75 to $85 because it is much less rare.

The graniteware items that follow are from the extensive collection and shop inventory of Gary and Lorraine Boggio of North Wind Antiques in Hennepin, Illinois.

The Boggios offer for sale one of the largest selections of pine furniture and graniteware in central Illinois. They may be contacted at:

North Wind Antiques
420 E. High St.
Hennepin, IL 61327
Telephone: (815) 925-7264

Measure with label. **$150–$190**

Dry measure. **$50–$75**

Salesman's sample wash basin. **$130–$150**

Straight measure. **$120–$140**

Child's plate and cup. **$40–$50**

Small teapot. **$140–$160**

Cups. **$18–$25 each**

"Gooseneck" two-cup coffeepot. **$175–$195**

Coffeepot. **$55–$75**

Large "gooseneck" pots. **$55–$125**

"Gooseneck" one-cup coffeepot. **$175–$225**

"Gooseneck" 1½-cup coffeepot. **$225–$250**

Coffeepots. **$90–$195 each**

Small "gooseneck" pots with biggins. **$225–$300 each**

Boston cream cans. **$75–$150**

Syrup pitcher. **$135–$140**

Water pitcher. **$160–$170**

Pitchers. **$160–$200 each**

Cloverleaf or beer pitcher. **$300–$350**

Small wash basin and pitcher. **$125–$150**

Milk pitchers. **$150–$165 each**

Large pitcher and bowl. **$190–$230**

Early pitcher and basin. **$175–$200**

Small measures. $175–$195 each

Small measures. $120–$165 each

Measures marked "Household." $65–$100

Fluted mold without a center post. $50–$65

Fluted tube pan. $75–$90

Fry pan with paper label. $60–$75

"Teardrop" sink strainer. $250–$275

Lunch box with lid marked "Cream City."
$200–$295

Percolator or "witch's hat." **$125–$140**

Small Nesco roaster. **$40–$75**

Sink strainer. **$215–$225**

Funnel with "Royal" label. **$65–$75**

Colander. **$35–$50**

Small funnels. **$65–$100 each**

Small pail with lid, stamped and dated. **$275–$350**

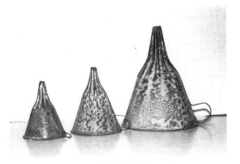

Elliptical funnels. **$50–$110 each**

Berry bucket with label. **$80–$100**

Large scoops. **$90–$120**

Oval batter kettle. **$220–$240**

Large bucket. **$55–$75**

Small cream cans. **$150–$225 each**

Coffee urn with label and cloth filter. **$350**

Chamber pot with label. **$140–$175**

Small berry buckets. **$125–$160 each**

Miner's dinner bucket. **$295**

Small batter jug. **$300–$325**

Turbin muffin pan. **$130–$140**

Beehive candlesticks. **$325–$450**

Muffin pan with wire edges. **$175–$200**

Salt box. **$600–$800**

Nine-hole muffin pan. **$75–$100**

Cuspidors. **$115–$125**

Dustpan. **$150–$160**

Gray and white Monarch gas stove. **$400–$450**

Large double boiler with cobalt trim. **$60**

Small double boiler with cobalt trim. **$75**

Pitcher and bowl with cobalt trim. **$120–$130**

Small berry bucket with cobalt trim. **$95**

Berry bucket with black trim. **$95**

"Gooseneck" one-cup coffeepot with black trim.
$150

Small milk pitcher with cobalt trim. **$75**

Syrup pitcher with cobalt trim. **$95**

Butter dish with cobalt trim. **$150**

Mug with cobalt trim. **$15**

Milk strainer. **$55**

Small berry bucket with cobalt trim and bail handle. **$80**

9 *Potpourri*

When we first started to collect antiques more than 25 years ago, the dealers described the dry sinks, pie safes, candlemolds, and decorated stoneware that we hunted almost nightly as "primitives." The concept of the antiques mall had not been explored to any degree in the 1960s and antiques shops flourished throughout middle America.

Almost all of the shops we frequented were advertised as "general line." The local dealers stocked glassware, dishes, oak furniture, and textiles. If they bought a house full of antiques, the primitives from the estate ended up in the basement or garage of their shop and our telephone usually rang.

In the early 1970s *country* became the adjective to describe the antiques we collected. The last 20 years have seen country slowly evolve in some areas into heart-shaped plywood key rings and cast concrete ducks.

Over the course of a year we travel to many antiques shows and markets and are almost as quick to write a check today when we find something as we were 20 years ago. It takes a little longer now to write the check because there are several more numbers involved than there used to be. The $350 dry sink is $2000 and the $60 "bird" crock is $575.

We originally decided that when we went to an antiques show we would not suffer the common malady of tunnel vision that often severely limits what you see. Basket collectors afflicted with this disease go to antiques shows and only look for their specialty. They can walk down an aisle, peer into a booth, and quickly move on if there are no baskets for sale that meet their standards. If they are asked later about a spectacular blue cupboard in a particular booth or the dealer and customer who engaged in a shouting match over a

piece of broken carnival glass, they have no memory of it because they neither saw nor heard it.

We have been interested in almost everything that falls within the general category of Americana from our first venture into the night in search of antiques. When we go to a show or market, we take a significant amount of time to look for painted furniture, holiday collectibles, advertising, decorated stoneware, baskets, Shaker, and kitchen-related antiques.

In several previous editions of this book we have included a chapter entitled Potpourri with pictures and prices of a wide variety of items that we have encountered during the course of our collecting and are of special interest to us.

The pictures, descriptions, and prices that follow carry on that tradition.

Tin measure, c. 1875–1900. **$20–$25**

Shaker hand mirror, c. late nineteenth century. **$110–$135**

*Blown-glass storage jar with tin lid, 9½" tall ×
4" diameter, c. 1880.* **$135–$150**

*Green leather fire bucket from New England, c.
mid-nineteenth century.* **$335–$400**

*Rare blown-glass storage jar with original tin
lid, 18" tall × 9" diameter, c. 1880.* **$500–
$575**

*Wrought-iron toaster, c. 1825–1850, Am-
erican.* **$275–$350**

Metal wall box for bills, used in a business office, English, c. 1900. **$40–$55**

Early nineteenth century pincushion with turned maple base painted blue, designed to be screwed to a table top, homespun cushion cover. **$200–$285**

Metal wall box for outgoing mail, probably English. **$30–$35**

Glass turkey candy dish, c. 1930. **$20–$28**

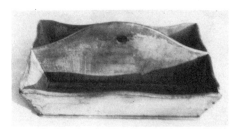

Dovetailed cherry knife and fork box, painted blue, c. 1840. **$275–$350**

Red-painted metal sewing storage kit, 8" in diameter, c. early twentieth century. $25–$30

Six-drawer tin spice box with lift lid storage area and original paint and stenciling, c. 1890–1910. $325–$375

Factory-made six-drawer tin spice chest with original gold paint and black lettering, c. 1890–1910. $300–$375

Six-drawer wooden spice box with original porcelain drawer pulls and lettering on drawers, c. early 1900s. $225–$250

Three Shaker pails with staved construction and metal bands, ranging in diameter from 4" to 7", all painted with white interiors. $275–$330 each

Shaker pail with "drop" or swing handle, 7" diameter, metal "diamond" braces on the sides, painted yellow with white interior, New England, c. early 1900s. **$300–$400**

Turned maple bowl, painted blue-green, 8" diameter, c. 1880–1900. **$175–$200**

Another view of turned maple bowl.

Blue-painted maple mixing bowl, 15" diameter, turned rather than hand-hewn. **$350–$425**

Apple butter bucket with original paper label and swing or "drop" handle with maple grip, staved construction with metal bands, painted gray, c. 1900. **$250–$300**

Shaker oval box with maple sides and pine top and bottom and brown paint, copper nails, 7" New England, nineteenth century. **$800–$1200**

Blue-painted sugar bucket with "drop" handle and staved construction, c. late-nineteenth century. $350–$400

Yellow-painted Shaker pine and maple butter or storage box with "button-hole" construction, 14" diameter, nineteenth century. $450–$550

Blue-painted butter tub with wooden bands and staved construction, 10" diameter × 11" high, c. 1870–1880. $275–$300

Red-painted unusual sugar bucket with "button-hole" hoops, nineteenth century, New England. $400–$500

Hand-hewn "work" bowl, painted brown, mid-nineteenth century. $300–$350

Red-painted Scandinavian storage box with cream colored initials and date "1831," 16" diameter. $300–$350

"Finger" construction measure with blue paint, 8" diameter, New England, nineteenth century.
$300–$375

Blue-painted pine bench with dovetailed sides, 30" long × 16" high, late nineteenth century.
$150–$200

Oversized pantry box with green paint and "drop" handle, 16" diameter, maple sides, pine top and bottom, nineteenth century. **$400–$500**

Detail view of the pine bench.

Unusual "Scandinavian" coffee grinder with red paint, brushed initials, c. 1860–1880.
$250–$325

Wall box with yellow paint, found in Kentucky, top of box made from lid of a candle box, late nineteenth century. **$150–$200**

Orange-painted butter churn with staved construction, "button-hole" hoops, "piggin" (a small stave extended upward as a handle), New England, mid-nineteenth century. **$500–$650**

Cast-iron coffee grinder, original painted surface, c. late nineteenth century. **$475–$600**

Hand-carved maple spoon, 11" long, probably nineteenth century, possibly European in origin. **$100–$125 if European; $275–$325 if American**

Pewter candleholder, c. mid-nineteenth century, possibly English in origin. **$100–$125**

Handwrought iron rushlight with candle socket, c. early nineteenth century. **$300–$350**

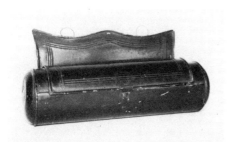

Hanging tin candle box with black paint, c. 1860s. **$275–$300**

Candle snuffer, c. 1890. **$45–$50**

Miniature kerosene lamp with pewter base, c. 1880–1900. **$100–$115**

186

Kerosene lamp designed for use with an iron wall bracket, late nineteenth-early twentieth century. **$70–$80**

Kerosene lamp, c. 1900–1925. **$75–$95**

Brass skimmer with handwrought iron handle, American (found in Pennsylvania), early nineteenth century. **$225–$300**

Galvanized watering can, c. 1950s. **$20–$25**

Crudely made brass dipper with wrought-iron handle, late nineteenth century, European in origin. **$60–$75**

Shaker clothes brush with turned maple handle and blue velvet cover, c. 1900, New England. **$150–$175**

Painted watering can, c. 1930–1950. **$45–$50**

Turned maple brush with lipstick red paint, c. late nineteenth century. **$250–$265**

Broom corn brush with turned maple handle, painted blue, c. 1840. **$175–$200**

Galvanized Tru-Value Hardware watering can, c. 1950. **$20–$25**

Artist's brush with maple handle, painted red at base, nineteenth century. **$40–$45**

Early twentieth century wisk broom with original blue paper cover. **$50–$75**

Patchwork crib quilt, early twentieth century.
$85–$125

Child's pine dish cupboard, 29" high × 14" wide, c. early 1900s. **$150–$175**

"Cows in the Clover" toy, complete with sound effects (activated by inverting and then righting the toy), c. 1925. **$30–$50**

Heavy wool child's stockings, c. 1880. **$20–$30 per pair**

Child's sled with heavy cast-iron runners, used for sliding on ice rather than snow, c. 1915, found in Michigan. **$550–$650**

Homemade black doll, c. 1880–1900. **$175–$225**

Horse pull toy on pine base, original condition, c. 1910, probably German in origin. **$200–$250**

Horse pull toy on pine base, probably German, c. 1910, original condition. **$200–$240**

Hand-carved jointed pine doll, c. early 1900s. **$175–$200**

Child's toy piano, c. 1930. **$75–$85**

Child's pine rocking chicken with red and blue paint, c. 1940. **$95–$115**

Child's suede boots, c. early twentieth century. **$55–$70**

Stuffed elephant toy, 38" tall, c. 1950. **$150–$200**

Homemade cat doll, c. 1940s. **$45–$60**

Cast-iron "W" windmill weight, c. early 1900s. **$275–$350**

Cast-iron cat bank, 5½" tall, c. early 1900s.
$75–$100

Cast-iron novelty bottle opener and "Dutch Maid" door knocker, c. 1920s, original painted finishes. Bottle opener, **$55–$70;** *door knocker,* **$40–$45.**

Cast "snow bird" used to hold snow on a slanted roof, c. 1875. **$75–$100**

"Hummer" windmill weight with painted finish, c. early 1900s. **$400–$450**

Birdhouses

In the early 1980s there was a national mania for collecting birdhouses. A problem that quickly became obvious was that a contemporary bird house left in the weather for three years closely resembles a bird house constructed in the 1930s or 1940s. This makes most "houses" extremely difficult to accurately date.

The mania has relaxed a bit in recent years but the market has been clouded a bit by folk art collectors who compete with country collectors for the more exotic bird houses with strong painted finishes and elaborate architectural detailing.

$100–$125

$100–$125

$125–$175

$35–$45

$60–$80

$200–$250

$50–$75

$30–$50

$125–$150

$35–$40

Country Baskets

Basket collectors face a variety of dilemmas in adding examples to their collections. A short list of difficulties includes the following.

1. Country baskets, like stoneware, were primarily utilitarian and not decorative. Most "working" baskets show signs of heavy use and rarely are found in mint condition.

2. Veneering machines and basket factories were commonly found in most areas of the United States after 1870. This gradually cut down the demand for hand-crafted baskets and fewer were made.

3. Handcrafted country baskets are difficult to accurately date because construction techniques changed little over many decades.

4. In the 1890s and early 1900s there was a craft revival in the United States. Basketmaking became popular for a brief period of time. These baskets sometimes are confused with the earlier utilitarian baskets.

5. Most baskets were constructed to be used for a variety of purposes. They may have made the trip to the general store for groceries or to the barn for eggs. To identify a specific use or date for a particular basket is a major challenge.

Wash basket with oak runners on the bottom, 30" long. **$200–$225**

Possibly Shaker-made storage basket. **$350–$425.** *The small handles would not allow anything of substance to be carried in the basket.*

Finely made miniature egg basket found in Pennsylvania. **$225–$250**

Indian-made blue-painted basket found in New England. **$300–$325**

Half or wall basket. $135–$150

Cheese basket, 14" diameter, used to separate the curds from the whey. $300–$375

Half or wall basket. $200–$250

Knife and fork basket, painted blue-green. $225–$275

Possibly a table basket used for storage. $200–$225

Open-weave drying basket. $275–$325

Rare handled rye straw basket found in Pennsylvania. **$250–$275**

Rye straw bread-rising basket from Pennsylvania. **$65–$70**

"Butt" or buttocks basket. **$235–$250**

Nantucket lightship basket with "drop" or swing handle. **$450–$575**

Turned wooden bottom of the Nantucket basket.

Garden or market basket with decorative colored splint. **$75–$100**

Gray-painted basket used for light chores or gathering eggs. **$150–$165**

Egg basket. **$135–$145**

Woven bottom of the light chores basket.

Swing-handled basket, probably used for gathering eggs. **$300–$375**

Raised or "kicked-in" bottom of the swing-handled basket.

Carved swing-handle.

Finely woven basket with slide lid; larger versions are called feather baskets. **$225–$250**

Swing-handled egg or gathering basket. **$275–$325**

Swing-handled basket, 7″ diameter. **$400–$475**

Close up showing how handle is attached to the basket.

Close up of basket.

Garden basket. **$150–$175**

Swing-handled basket, 14" diameter, "kicked in" or raised bottom. **$400–$450**

Egg basket, painted bittersweet or orange, 10" diameter. **$300–$325**

Close up of basket.

Table basket with carved handles and splayed sides, used for storage. **$135–$175**

Gathering basket, possibly of Shaker-made manufacture, with oval top and rectangular bottom. **$300–$375**

Miniature egg basket in "melon" form. **$150–$175**

Open-weave herb gathering basket. **$275–$325**

Unique egg basket painted green on the exterior and blue on the interior, extremely well made with unusual handle. **$375–$425**

Factory-made wash basket painted a strong blue, c. 1900–1925. **$175–$225**

Tightly woven "butt" or buttocks basket. **$225–$275**

Egg or gathering basket. **$100–$135**

Ball of oak splint used to make baskets. **$15–$20**

Holiday Collectibles

"Forget me not" valentine, 4" × 3", mid-nineteenth century, found in Pennsylvania. **$100–$135**

Christmas tree made of chicken feathers, 40" tall, c. 1920s, original painted base, German in origin. **$275–$350**

Framed basket of flowers. **$75–$100**

Rare paper Halloween lantern with ears. **$250–$275**

Pressed-paper Easter rabbit made by F.N. Burt Company, Buffalo, N.Y., 6¹/₂" tall, c. 1930–1940s. **$55–$60**

Pressed-paper Easter rabbit, Drake Process, c. 1930–1940s, 9" tall. **$55–$60**

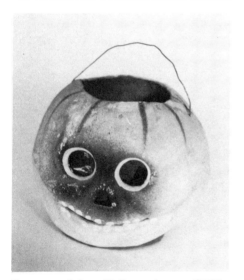

Rare paper skeleton Halloween lantern. **$250– $300**

Pressed paper "devil" Halloween lantern, c. 1940s to early 1950s. **$125–$175**

Pressed paper lantern, c. 1940s. **$55–$65**

Uncommon pressed-paper black cat, Halloween lantern. **$75–$85**

Pressed paper lantern, c. 1950s. **$60–$80**

Full figured Jack-o-lantern, c. 1940s. **$125–$150**

Paper witch container for Halloween candy, c. 1940s. **$25–$30**

"Trick or Treat" metal lantern, c. 1950s. **$20–$25**

Halloween candy or cookie tin, c. 1940s. **$35–$50**

Pressed-paper Jack-o-lantern, c. 1940s. **$60–$80**

Halloween Noisemakers from the 1940s and 1950s

$10–$14

$15–$18

$20–$24

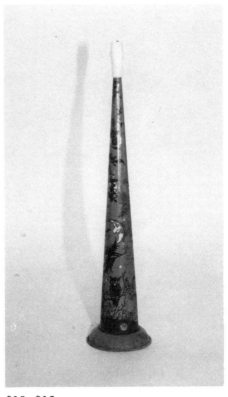

$10–$13

$9–$12

$10–$14

$10–$14

10 *Woodworking Tools*

The section that follows was put together by Dr. Bill Smith, a veteran collector of tools for many years. He may be contacted at:

Dr. Bill Smith
P.O. Box 19
Savoy, IL 61874

During the last 20 years tool collecting has expanded at a very fast rate. In fact, it has been estimated that there are at least 70,000 to 80,000 serious tool collectors in the United States. That is one of the reasons tool prices have been increasing each year.

Currently there are at least 35 major tool collecting organizations in the United States. There are also some tool organizations that are international in scope. Listed on the following page are the names and addresses of two major associations.

Mid-West Tool Collectors Association
P.O. Box 6
Naylor, MO 63951

Early American Industries Association
P.O. Box 2128
Albany, NY 12220

As tool collecting became more popular, a standard grading system was needed to evaluate tools. *Fine Tool Journal* developed the standards which are now widely accepted by tool collectors throughout the United States. The price of a tool is based on its condition according to this standard and its degree of rarity. Following is the grading standard formulated by the *Fine Tool Journal*.

There are thousands of collectible tools on the market today. The pictures that follow are a representative sampling of the tools that are available to collectors.

CONDITION CLASSIFICATION   MANUFACTURED / METAL TOOLS*

CATEGORY	USABLE	FINISH	WEAR	REPAIR	RUST	MISC.
new	totally	100%	none	none	none	+ orig. pkg.
fine	totally	90–100%	minimal	none	trace	
good +	yes	75–90%	normal	minor or none	light	some dings or scratch OK
good	yes	50–75%	norm.-mod.	minor	light	minor chips
good -	probably	30–50%	mod.-hvy.	correct	mod.	chips OK
fair	no	0–30%	excessive	major	mod.-hvy.	
poor	no	n/a	excessive	damaged	heavy	

CONDITION CLASSIFICATION   PRIMITIVE OR WOODEN TOOLS

CATEGORY	USABLE	FINISH	WEAR	REPAIR	RUST
fine	yes	appropriate	normal	minor	light
good +	yes	appropriate	normal	correct	light
good	yes	appropriate	normal	correct	moderate
good -	probably	needs work	moderate	may need	mod./heavy
fair	maybe	probably not	heavy	major or damaged	heavy

* copyright *Fine Tool Journal*

Stanley No. 5C plane in like-new condition with the original box. **$75–$100**

Stanley No. 95 edge trimming block plane in the box with decal. **$150–$225**

Stanley No. A45 aluminum combination plow plane, rarest of the 45 series. **$2000–$3000**

Sargent V-B-M No. 1068 tongue and groove plane. **$75–$125**

Stanley No. S18 steel block plane in original box, mint condition. **$250–$300**

Center brass wheel screw-arm plow plane with ivory tips. **$2000–$3000**

Sargent No. 1080 and 1085 combination planes. $200–$250

Left to right: Stanley 3X handle and 5X handle, $10–$15 each; Stanley No. A6, $150–$200; Stanley No. A4, $100–$150; Stanley No. A5, $125–$175.

Left to right: Sargent No. 407 smoothing plane, $80–$125; Sargent No. 507 rabbet block plane, $125–$200; Sargent No. 707 auto-set, $600–$700.

Clockwise from top: beech groove plane, $15–$30; beechwood smoothing plane, $15–$30; round molding plane, $15–$25; hollow double iron plane, $20–$30.

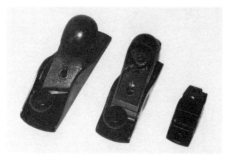

Left to right: Stanley No. 140 rabbet block plane, $60–$90; Stanley No. 203 block plane, $15–$30; Stanley No. 101 block plane, $20–$30.

Stanley No. 46 Traut's Patent adjustable dado, fillester, and plow plane, in original box with cutters. $250–$350

Stanley No. 248A Weather Strip in original box, mint condition. **$175–$225**

Stanley No. 83 wood scraper with roller. **$40–$75**

Salesman's sample Stanley No. 20 with cut-away, very rare. **$300–$400**

Stanley No. 40 chisels. **$15–$30 each**

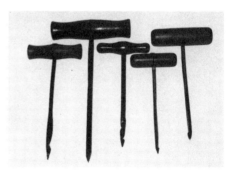

Hand adze. **$55–$150**

Various types and sizes of gimlets. **$5–$15 each**

Maple workbench with double vise. **$400–$600**

Various styles of hoop drivers. **$10–$15 each**

Rare set of cooper's stave gaugers. **$80–$100**

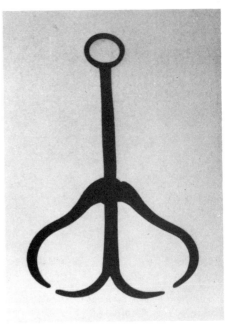

A small set of blacksmith's double calipers. **$30–$60**

Cooper's V-croze of brass and English oak, "B.F. Horn, E. St. Louis, Il. No. 101." $60–$95

Coachmaker's router (top), $25–$40; traveler made by a blacksmith, $30–$50.

Set of Sargent V-B-M Russell Jenning's pattern bits. $70–$90

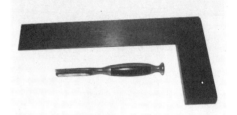

Sargent T square, $20–$30; rare Sargent rosewood handle gouge, $45–$55.

Complete Winchester tool chest, very rare. $3000–$5000

Top to bottom: Stanley No. 80 scraper, $10–$15; spokeshaves, $5–$15 each; Stanley No. 67 universal spokeshave, $30–$75.

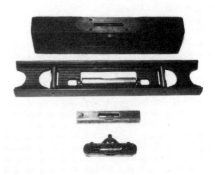

Top to bottom: Stanley No. 102 cherry level, $10–$30; Stanley No. 36 iron level, $15–$30; Stanley No. 38 one-half level, $20–$30; Stanley No. 4 pocket level, $15–$20.

Top: Stanley No. 59 doweling tool, $30–$50; left to right: Stanley No. 97 marking gauge, $10–$20; Stanley No. 49 bit-gauge, $10–$20; Stanley No. 4 trammels, $25–$45.

Clockwise from left: burl mallet, $15–$30; walnut clapboard marking gauge, $25–$50; beech spokeshave, $10–$20; wood marking gauge, $15–$20.

11

Auction Houses, Group Shops, and Antiques Markets

When we first began buying American country antiques, most of what we found was purchased from antiques shops located in small towns or in the basements of private homes. The dealers generally were kind to us because we were young and enthusiastic. We are still enthusiastic.

Four or five nights a week we would attempt to add to our collection by traveling within a 100-mile radius of our home in the middle of Illinois. If the front light was on at most of the dealers' homes, they were open for business.

About 45 minutes away was a rural community that had a large grain elevator and a small antiques shop. There was also a restaurant that offered an all-you-can-eat buffet on Friday evenings for $1. The owner of the local antiques shop was the widow of the former town physician. She regularly attended farm auctions to keep busy and had her shop in her late husband's office. She especially liked painted dry sinks and blanket boxes and priced her purchases only a few dollars above what she had paid. Many times she urged us to buy a particular piece because "eventually you will have a place to put it."

At that point there were no antiques malls or group shops with multiple dealers in our immediate area. It was standard procedure for us to go antiquing by traveling from town to town and shop to shop in search of Americana.

The rising cost of gas, a declining number of shops as dealers grew old and retired or died, increased prices, and a decreasing supply of quality merchandise all worked together to change the way most of us went antiquing in the late 1970s and 1980s.

Group shops made up of several dealers with similar interests began to appear and prosper. Antiques malls or markets that provided space for rent to dealers who could not offer all their attention all the time to selling antiques also became popular and met a need for collectors. Now it was possible to see a large variety and quality of merchandise offered for sale in a relatively confined area.

In addition to the growth of multiple dealer antiques shops and malls, regional auction houses that offer periodic cataloged sales of Americana have become an increasingly important source for buying antiques.

Copake Country Auctions

Michael Fallon is an auctioneer and appraiser who conducts cataloged Americana auction sales of formal and country furniture, Shaker items, quilts, coverlets, hooked rugs, samplers, and folk art. He is a member of the National Association of Certified Auctioneers, National Auctioneers Association, New England Appraisers Association, and the International Society of Appraisers.

The items that follow have been sold recently at Copake Country Auctions. Mr. Fallon may be contacted at:

Mr. Michael Fallon
Copake Country Auctions
Box H
Copake, NY 12516
Telephone: (518) 329-1142

Cherry secretary, $775; four bird cage Windsor chairs, $1050 set.

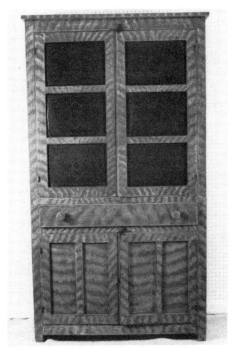

Paint-decorated pie safe. **$1000**

Dutch cupboard, c. 1840. **$1400**

Contemporary wooden Indian, **$650;** *cupboard from a hotel,* **$650.**

Two-piece step-back cupboard, nineteenth century. **$1550**

Two-piece cupboard with arched door, $1450; two-piece corner cupboard, c. 1820, $1000.

Set of one-half spindle plank-seat chairs. $85 each

Painted cupboard from a country store. $2425

Set of arrow-back plank-seat chairs from Pennsylvania, nineteenth century. $80 each

Child's twig rocking chair, **$95;** *Pilgrim-style child's high chair,* **$325.**

Pennsylvania deacon's bench. **$650**

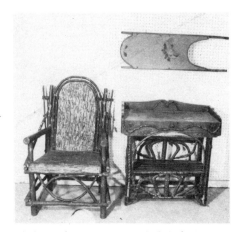

Clockwise from top: painted sled, $60; twig planter, $385; twig armchair, $200.

Eighteenth-century theorem. **$1375**

Fraktur with Masonic motif dated "1804." **$1750**

Folk art cane from New York State. **$325**

Pencil drawing by itinerant New York State folk artist Fritz Vogt. **$1250**

Calligraphy signed "F.B. Hoyman" and dated "1875." **$550**

Watercolor painting attributed to J.A. Davis, early nineteenth century. **$770**

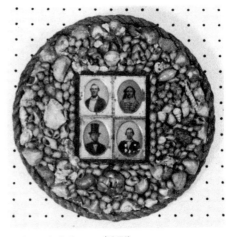

Sailor's shell frame. **$375**

"B.W. Dudley, M.D." by Aug. Edouart.
$1150

Miniature oil on paper, nineteenth century.
$225

"Reward of Merit" by Joseph Kratzer, 1841.
$550

Penmanship sample (calligraphy), nineteenth century. **$300**

"Celebrated Hobo Band" litho, early twentieth century. **$125**

Hooked rug featuring a dog and a cat. **$500**

Framed hook rug of a farm scene. **$550**

Wood carving of a horse, nineteenth century. **$350**

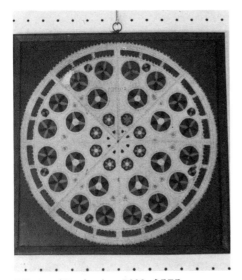

"Cut work" valentine, 1822. **$575**

Folk art smoking pipe. **$400**

Weathervane made from license plates. **$275**

The Rover toy gunboat. **$550**

Collection of mechanical toys, left to right: chicken and cart, **$40;** *cat and ball,* **$40;** *bellhop,* **$70;** *monkey ballplayer,* **$20.**

Tin toys: "Betty," **$150**; *"Range Rider,"* **$90.**

Santa Claus tin toy. **$1200**

Halloween paper collectibles. **$90 set**

Ohio tin fire truck. **$525**

233

Buddy L sand and gravel truck. **$2000**

Baby carriage, c. 1870. **$225**

Rip Van Winkle cast metal clock. **$250**

Country Village Antiques

Country Village Antiques of Glendora, California, is a cooperative shop owned by 16 dealers who specialize in early Americana. The "Village" contains 4,000 square feet of country antiques in room settings. Glendora is 25 miles east of downtown Los Angeles.

The Country Village has a large open house in early November and one in June. Shop hours are 10 A.M. to 5 P.M. Monday through Saturday and 11 A.M. to 4 P.M. on the last Sunday of each month. The mailing address is:

Country Village Antiques
163 N. Glendora Avenue
Glendora, CA 91740
Telephone: (818) 914-2542,
(818) 914-6860

"Tin kitchen" with spit, c. mid-1800s. **$650**

Collection of twentieth-century children's drums, **$49–$85 each;** *set of children's blocks, 1920s,* **$155.**

Large field basket, unusual size, excellent original condition. **$125**

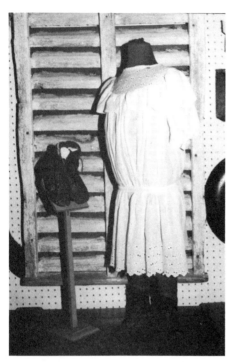

Metal barn found in Iowa with old red and black paint. $125

Window vent from an Ohio barn with old blue paint, $225; shoe display stand, $58; pair of boy's shoes, $65; child's mannequin and dress, $595.

Painted pedal horse made in 1927 by John Pierce for his 3-year-old granddaughter for Christmas. $895

Children's twig rocking chair with old green paint. $300

German horse on wheels, c. 1890. **$795**

Primitive dappled gray rocking horse with log body, c. mid-1800s. **$925**

Unusual iron candle sconce with painted floral decoration, c. late 1800s. **$185**

Doll house and matching fence from Pennsylvania, c. 1915. **$250**

Carnival game targets from Louisiana, 1930s. **$295**

Ash splint "gizzard" basket in original finish and condition with a double-rapped rim. **$695**

Pine and oak wagon with original red paint and stenciled horse decoration. **$895**

Handmade dollhouse made from cigar boxes, with green glass windows, found in Wisconsin. **$900**

Barn with steeple, c. 1940s, **$130;** *old barn found in Pennsylvania,* **$155.**

Shaker rocking chair with black stained finish, Mt. Lebanon, N.Y. **$1500**

Maple tilt-top table, c. mid-1800s. **$325**

Cast-iron tea kettle with "gooseneck" spout, c. late 1800s. **$485**

Wrought iron "fire dogs," c. 1800. **$225 pair**

Red and white Christmas tree fence with clothespin posts, c. 1850–1900. **$225**

Wrought iron hanging trammel candleholder, c. early 1800s. **$895**

Creekside Antiques

Creekside Antiques is located 20 minutes north of San Francisco, California, in the small community of San Anselmo. Creekside Antiques is a cooperative or group shop with 15 dealers who specialize in Americana, country furniture, pottery, and early textiles. Additional information may be secured by contacting:

Creekside Antiques
241 Sir Francis Drake
San Anselmo, CA 94960
Telephone: (415) 457-1266

Stenciled and mustard-painted side chairs, c. 1830s. **$375 each**

Late nineteenth-century toy cart. **$1100**

Sheraton cherry chest of drawers. **$1400**

Early butter churn with original red paint.
$350

Tramp art bureau box. **$650**

Days Gone By Antiques

Days Gone By Antiques was established in 1972 by Tom and Nancy Benda and was one of the first multi-dealer shops in the Midwest at that time.

The shop specializes in fine-quality country furniture and primitives, along with related collectibles and clocks. The shop is located in Frankfort, Illinois, centrally located two miles south of Interstate 80 on Route 45 and one-half mile north of Route 30. Days Gone By Antiques is open Tuesday to Saturday from 11 A.M. until 5 P.M.

Days Gone By Antiques
20555 LaGrange Rd.
Frankfort, IL 60423
Telephone: (815) 469-1908

Mixed woods (cherry, walnut, and oak) schoolmaster's desk with wood peg construction, c. 1850. **$450–$595**

Maple child's rocker with woven splint seat, c. 1910, **$125–$150;** *oak and ash kitchen chair, c. 1889,* **$550–$695 set of six.**

Wardrobe with ornate rose incised carving, c. 1890. **$1700–$2000**

Maple 2-piece step-back cupboard, c. 1910. **$1095–$1295**

Small pine kitchen table with drawer and two-board top, c. 1890, **$300–$400**; large turned wood bowl, c. 1900, **$95.**

Handmade pine country kitchen work center with lift top, c. 1880. **$450–$525**

Oak stool, pine crock bench, and pine three-legged milk stool, c. 1890. **$75–$90 each**

Original grained finish pine kitchen pantry cabinet, c. 1883. **$800–$1000**

Child's pressed back rocker, c. 1870. **$225–$350**

Ornate oak rocker from Norway, c. 1890. **$375–$450**

Immigrant's pine trunk, c. 1870. **$300–$395**

Handmade yarn winder with wooden gears, c. 1870. **$150–$250**

New Haven regulator clock with oak case, c. 1905. **$325–$375**

Walnut handmade knife tray, c. 1870. **$65–$75**

Iron park bench, c. 1880. **$295–$350**

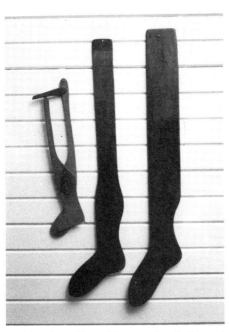

Child's adjustable stocking stretcher, lady's and man's stretchers. **$35–$55 each**

Wooden salt box, c. 1890. **$85–$125**

Boot company sign with original paint, c. late 1880s. **$295–$350**

Chicago Stamping Company advertising match holder with original artwork, c. 1890. **$65–$85**

Advertising sign with writing on both sides, sand paint, and gold lettering, c. 1920. **$450–$600**

Tin templates for cutting patterns for quilts, c. 1850. **$65–$95 each**

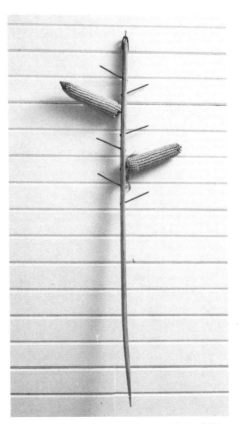

Primitive wooden corn drier, c. 1880. **$55–$75**

Tin graters, c. 1900. **$30–$70 each**

Wooden graters, c. 1880s. $65–$85 **each**

Wooden shovel made from one piece of wood, c. 1870. **$95–$125**

Potato planter, c. 1900, **$40–$55;** *handmade iron chain trammel, c. 1870,* **$95–$150.**

Handmade candle snuffer, c. late 1800s. **$25– $55**

Double-blade food chopper, c. 1900; five-blade chopper, c. 1886; **$25–$35 each**

Iron and brass lawn sprinkler and iron Christmas tree stand with original green/gold paint, c. 1890. **$28–$40**

Kerosene lamps: brass collar with iron base and finger lamp, c. 1850s. **$65–$90 each**

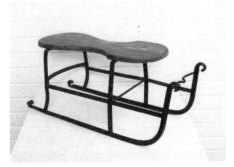

Sears #11 New Star painted potbelly stove, c. 1910. **$300–$400**

Handmade child's sled with iron base and original red paint, c. 1880. **$200–$300**

Pulver chewing gum machine with policeman holding stop/go sign. **$550–$800**

Fishtail balance scale with weights and original red paint, c. 1890. **$150–$225**

Adjustable pine quilt rack, c. 1880. **$35–$60**

Challenger Hot Mix Nuts machine, c. 1910. **$195–$300**

Three-part pewter calla lily ice cream mold, rose mold, and small floral pattern mold, c. 1890. **$55–$65 each**

Balance scale #80, C.W.S. manchester. **$175–$225**

Red Wing water crock and Red Wing self-draining crock, c. late 1800s. **$300–$400 each**

Collapsible auto water carrier, c. 1910. **$25–$40**

Graniteware coffeepot and tin coffeepot, c. 1890. **$55–$75 each**

Graniteware coffeepots, left to right: 2-quart brown and white pot with tin lid, mottled gray pot with tin lid, and blue and white pot, c. 1900. **$60–$115 each**

Lancaster Antiques Market

The Lancaster Antiques Market is located in Lancaster, Kentucky, near Shakertown at Pleasant Hill. The mall contains more than 20,000 square feet of Americana and is open from 10 A.M. to 5 P.M. Mondays through Saturdays and from 1 P.M. to 5 P.M. on Sundays. For a fee of $10, the Lancaster Antiques Market offers a narrated videotape of items that currently are for sale. Antiques are shipped daily via United Parcel Service (UPS) or freight.

Rose Holtzclaw and Ellen Tatem, owners of the market, also have a restored nineteenth-century bed and breakfast furnished with antiques that is used by visiting dealers and collectors.

Lancaster Antiques Market
102 Hamilton Avenue
Lancaster, KY 40444
Telephone: (606) 792-4536

Primitive high chair in mustard paint. **$95**

Early Kentucky chair with hickory splint seat. **$85**

Two-drawer cherry chest only 17" high with dovetailed sides and chamfered back. **$295**

Shaker rocker with replaced seat. **$450**

Child's chair, **$125**; *early blue wool socks,* **$75**.

Pine and poplar high chair with dark brown paint and splayed leg construction. **$250**

252

Chicken rock, used to collect rainwater for chickens. $65

Decorated metal wheelbarrow. $195

Stoneware canning jar signed "McCarthy and Bayless, Louisville." $350

Large painted pine finial from stair post in nineteenth-century Kentucky home. $145

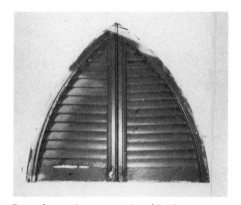

Barn shutter in green paint. **$145**

Pewter charger, 14½" diameter. **$325**

Stone fruit. **$35 each**

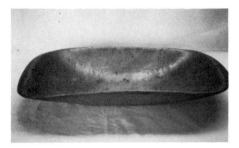

Dough bowl with 20" diameter, much wear, natural finish. **$125**

Divided box in green paint with dovetailed sides. **$145**

Candle box in green paint 16" wide, **$185**; *candle box in natural finish, 12",* **$65**.

Wooden mold in mustard and red paint. **$95**

Large basket in green paint with wooden runners on the bottom. **$195**

Wall hanging basket in blue paint with red trim. **$65**

Unusual basket with flat side for hanging by it side, double-wrapped top and "kicked-up" bottom. **$395**

Large splint basket. **$165**

Small Shaker picnic basket, 5", $195; Shaker brush, $135.

Oval pantry box with straight seams and wooden pegs. **$335**

Wooden carrier with straight seams and a natural finish, 9½" diameter. **$150**

Pantry box in mustard paint with mouse hole. **$265**

Shaker oval boxes with fingers: 7" box, $495; 11½" box, $695.

Firkin or sugar bucket in green paint. **$125**

Small doll trunk with early wallpaper. **$150**

Large pantry box in red paint with a fingered lid. **$295**

Carrier in mustard paint with fingered lid.
$395

Round pantry box, 15" diameter. **$895**

Joy Luke Auction Gallery

The Joy Luke Auction Gallery is an auction and appraisal company that conducts estate and consignment cataloged auctions and specialized sales throughout the year. They feature estate jewelry, Indian artifacts, dolls, toys, textiles, and furniture. The Joy Luke auctioneers are members of the National Auctioneers Association and the Illinois State Auctioneers Association.

Joy Luke's commission is 20 percent, and all items are fully insured. Catalogs, mailing lists, and additional information may be secured by contacting:

Joy Luke Auction Gallery
300 E. Grove Street
Bloomington, IL 61702
Telephone: (309) 828-5533

Lionel illuminated station #124 marked "Lionel City" with original box and minor scratch on roof, **$340**; *Lionel illuminated signal tower #438 with original box,* **$325.**

Very early painted tin toy engine with cast-iron wheels and friction movement. **$150**

Large tin trolley car marked "Rapid Transit" with friction movement, 20" long. **$325**

Two cast metal Civil War soldier figures, 7¼" high. **$200 pair**

Very early cast-iron toy steam engine, 2" high × 5½" long. **$90**

American Flyer train set consisting of engine #302, tender, gondola, refrigerator car, gas tank car, caboose, track, 45-watt transformer, instruction book, all original boxes (engine and tender shown). **$70**

Lionel track cleaner car #3927 in orange and black with two Lionel track cleaning fluid containers, **$125;** *Lionel Rio Grande snowplow #53 in black and yellow with original box,* **$325.**

Early cast-iron horse and buggy. **$140**

Lionel standard gauge crane car #219, marked "Lifting Capacity 20 Tons," with original box marked "No. 219 Derrick." **$1200**

Early painted tin horse pull toy, **$110;** *small tin horse pull toy,* **$90.**

Early cast metal toy with horses pulling sleigh bells, c. 1870, mounted on wooden stand. **$350**

Child's rocking horse on wooden stand with red vinyl saddle, black fabric fur, and silk mane and tail. **$250**

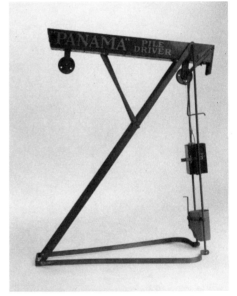

Early "Panama Pile Driver" tin toy. **$100**

John Henry Belter "Rosalie" pattern chair. **$8000 for a pair**

Victorian walnut wall shelf with comb drawer and words "God Bless Our Home." **$125**

Sixteen medals on ribbons, including Purple Heart and political medals. **$130**

Royal Doulton "Captain Hook" character jugs 6¼" high and 4" high. **$425 (large) and $340 (small)**

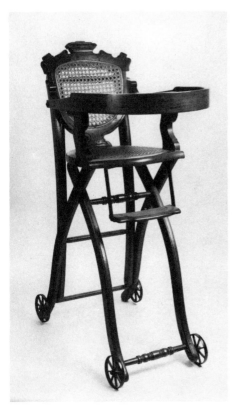

One of four side chairs with demi arms from Victorian walnut parlor set that included a loveseat, gentleman's chair, and lady's chair. **$3000 for the set**

Victorian walnut and burl wood high/low chair with cane seat and back. **$550**

Royal Doulton character jug entitled "The Clown," white hair, 6¼" high. **$850**

Early small spinning wheel in working condition. **$400**

Early American cherry long case clock with painted metal face decorated with flowers, 87" high × 19½" wide, calendar movement, roman numerals, second sweep hand, brass finials, brass works stamped "Birmingham," c. 1790. **$6600**

Buffalo Pottery Deldare Ware: #166 two-handled cake plate with scene entitled "Ye Village Gossips," signed "M. Gerhardt," 1909, 11¼" across, **$600**; #196 3-piece tea set with scene entitled "Village Life in Olden Days," 1909, **$900**; #106 fruit bowl with scene entitled "Ye Village Tavern," signed "Sayo," 1908, 9" diameter. **$450**

Buffalo Pottery Deldare Ware: #116 dresser tray with scene entitled "Dancing Ye Minuet," signed "L. Winter," 1909, 9″ × 12″, minor chips, $275; #206 tea set with scene entitled "Village Life in Ye Olden Days" with 4¾″ teapot signed "H. Ford," covered sugar signed "N. Sheehan," and creamer signed "L.N.," four signed cups and saucers signed and dated 1909, $650; #136 chocolate cup with village scene, signed "M.A.D.," $400.

Walt Disney Mickey Mouse lidded cookie jar, 10″ high. $130

Midwest Country Antiques

Midwest Country Antiques is a group shop owned by Larry and Pat Coughlin and Darrell and Lana Potter. It is located between Terre Haute, Indiana, and St. Louis, Missouri, on Interstate 70 in downtown St. Elmo, Illinois, an oil boomtown of the 1930s. The shop is open daily, Monday through Saturday, from 9 A.M. to 5 P.M. and on Sundays by appointment. The shop specializes in American country antiques.

Additional information may be obtained by contacting:

Darrell and Lana Potter
RR 2
Box 193
St. Elmo, IL 62458
Telephone: (618) 829-5471

Handcrafted log cabin doll house, early twentieth century. $350

*Spice chests (left to right): green chest, **$385**; blue chest, **$390**; salmon chest, **$325**.*

*Rope bed with dark blue paint, early nineteenth century. **$950***

*Blue-green Amish wash bench with unusual carved feet. **$175***

*Painted maple and poplar pie safe, late nineteenth century. **$650–$800***

*Child- or doll-size pine chest with green stiles. **$235***

Painted pine document storage box marked "1864," slide top. **$335**

Butter mold with "Suss-Rahmbutter (Sweet Cream Butter)" and the initials "A.O." **$425**

Rag dolls, $75–$125 each; doll-size red stenciled chair, $75; small doll with celluloid face, $35.

Firemark from an insurance company indicating that a particular structure was insured. **$260**

Teddy bear, $350; doll-size rocking chair, $85; green-painted buttocks basket, $185.

Painted oak splint baskets, nineteenth century.
$145 each

Splint basket, early twentieth century. **$65–$85**

Yellow-painted splint basket with varnished finish. **$165**

Refinished maple chopping bowl, 15" long. **$85–$100**

Antiques and Americana

Dick and Kay Thompson are dealers in advertising and Americana who do not maintain an "open" shop. They are especially interested in early twentieth-century Coca-Cola-related items and thermometers and are constantly seeking items to add to their collection and inventory.

The Thompsons may be contacted at:

Dick and Kay Thompson
320 E. Washington St.
Pontiac, IL 61764
Telephone: (815) 842-2586

Coca-Cola Tray Chronology

Coca-Cola trays were used in soda fountains and restaurants to serve customers and advertise a product that was constantly growing in popularity. The early trays (from 1897 to the mid-1920s) featured fashionably dressed women holding a glass of the beverage. From 1925 until the early 1960s, the trays displayed equally well-dressed women with a bottle of Coca-Cola rather than a glass.

Coca-Cola Trays

1897–1902   *only* round trays were made

1903–1910   oval trays and round trays were made

1910–1921   *only* oval and rectangular trays were made

after 1921   *only* rectangular trays were made

Change or Tip Trays—made between 1900 and 1920

1900–1906   round trays
1907–1920   oval trays

It is not unusual to find a change or tip tray in heavily used condition because most became ashtrays or coasters and suffered the consequences over the years. Rarely is a change or tip tray in pristine condition discovered.

Coca-Cola tray, 1948. **$150–$200**

Coca-Cola tray, 1920. **$500–$600**

Coca-Cola tray, 1938. **$200–$250**

Coca-Cola trays, from top left: 1917, $275–$325; 1914, $400–$500; 1920, $375–$575.

Coca-Cola tray, 1950. $75–$100

Coca-Cola trays, clockwise from top left: 1912, $400–$500; 1909, $450–$600; 1904, $500–$700.

Coca-Cola thermometer, 1942. $300–$450

Coca-Cola thermometers, from left: 1936, $250–$300; 1950, $100–$125; 1939, $200–$250.

Sauer's Flavoring thermometer, c. 1918. $650–$900

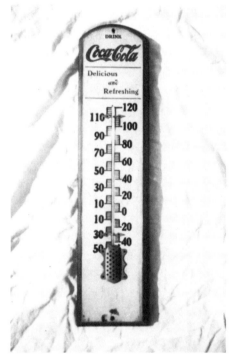

Coca-Cola thermometer, c. 1915. $750–$850

Hill's Brothers Coffee thermometer, c. 1920s. $650–$800

Final Examination

The recent articles in several semi-scholarly journals about this examination replacing ACT or SAT scores for entrance into major universities or barber colleges are probably not true.

The following material is critical to any future success you might achieve. Please read slowly. Pay *special* attention to direction #6 below.

When you hold your right forefinger on the circular area marked "Press" and count to seven by twos, your thumb print will be electronically locked into our national computer. This will assure that your score will *not* be made available to the several finance companies seeking your new address or groups demanding donors for genetic experiments.

Directions

1. Read each question carefully.

2. There is *usually* only one correct response.

3. If this test is taken on anything other than a flat surface, the book *may* dissolve.

4. Do not seek any assistance from blood relatives.

5. If you dial 700-ANTIQUE, after the moaning stops a person will be available to answer your questions. Do *not* tell him/her that you are alone or that you enjoy *National Geographic.*

6. If you cannot read, stay where you are and someone will arrive shortly to assist you. If the person that shows up has red hair, *do not ask* him/her any questions about the scar.

Matching

Match the lettered items (at right) with the numbered items (at left).

_____ 1. comb-back

_____ 2. incised

_____ 3. oak

_____ 4. till

_____ 5. molded

_____ 6. Bennington, Vermont

_____ 7. walnut

_____ 8. Wallace Nutting

_____ 9. pine

_____ 10. cobalt

_____ 11. dovetailed

_____ 12. refinished pine pie safe with "geometric" tins

_____ 13. mahogany

_____ 14. ovoid

_____ 15. fired at more than 2300°F

a. stoneware

b. describes most stoneware made after 1900

c. redware

d. used to glaze stoneware

e. author of the definitive book on American woodenware

f. location of weekend antiques markets

g. $3000 to $5000 (value)

h. pine was sometimes grained to resemble this wood

i. wood of choice for Victorian cabinetmakers

j. type of Windsor chair

k. an imported wood not native to America

l. small box inside a blanket chest

m. pear shaped

n. site of famous nineteenth-century pottery

o. coloring agent used to decorate stoneware

_____ 16. Gould

_____ 17. blue painted "open" pine cupboard

_____ 18. Adamstown, Pa

_____ 19. rock salt

_____ 20. had to be glazed to be watertight

p. $500 to $650 (value)

q. most commonly used wood to make "country" furniture

r. author who produced a line of colonial reproduction furniture in the early 1900s

s. technique used to join two pieces of wood at a corner

t. earliest technique used to decorate American stoneware

True-False

21. This blanket box is constructed of pine.

True False

22. The blanket box would date from *before* 1885.

True False

23 In red paint the blanket box is worth a *minimum* of $800.

True False

24. Stripped and refinished, the blanket box is worth a *minimum* of $275.

True False

25. In blue paint the blanket box is worth a *minimum* of $575.

True False

26. In carefully studying the picture of the blanket box, it is readily apparent that the box is American and *not* European in origin.

True False

27. This is a molded piece of American stoneware.

True False

28. It dates from about 1830.

True False

29. It has a value of *more* than $150.

    True   False

30. It was made in Bloomington, Illinois, for the Sleepy Eye Milling Company of Sleepy Eye, Minnesota.

    True   False

31. Most American stoneware made after the 1830s was molded rather than hand-thrown on a potter's wheel.

    True   False

32. The handle on the lunch box could be described as a "drop" or bail handle.

    True   False

33. Abraham Lincoln *could* have carried this lunch container to Ford's Theater with a light snack on an April night in 1865.

    True   False

34. The wooden grip on the handle of the lunch box is made of black walnut.

    True   False

35. The value of this lunch box is *less* than $45.

    True   False

36. Before sailing on the *Titanic* in 1912, a passenger could have gone into a store and purchased this lunch box.

    True   False

37. The two irons and the trivet are made of cast bronze.

    True   False

38. The irons date from the eighteenth century and the trivet dates from about 1850.

    True   False

39. The two irons and the trivet have a total value of at *least* $150.

    True   False

40. Most American Windsor chairs were made from several different kinds of wood.

    True   False

41. Most American Windsor chairs were painted red or blue.

    True   False

42. The Windsor chair is an American invention.

    True   False

43. The chair is named for Melville Windsor, who designed the first example at his chair factory in Springfield, Massachusetts, in the mid-1700s.

True   False

44. The Shakers made and sold rocking chairs in eight sizes well into the twentieth century.

True   False

45. A glazed cupboard usually has several "lights."

True   False

Essay Question (5 points)

Trace the origins of the step-back cupboard. In your answer be sure to note the contributions made by Alexander Graham Bell and Cecil Sckell. It is important that the basic rules of punctuation and English grammar be faithfully observed. Do *not* allude to the tragedy of the falling piano bench on May 12, 1943 in any portion of your response.

Answers

1. j	16. e	31. False
2. t	17. g	32. True
3. h	18. f	33. False
4. l	19. d	34. False
5. b	20. c	35. False
6. n	21. True	36. True
7. i	22. True	37. False
8. r	23. False	38. False
9. q	24. True	39. False
10. o	25. True	40. True
11. s	26. False	41. False
12. p	27. True	42. False
13. k	28. False	43. False
14. m	29. True	44. True
15. a	30. False	45. True

Interpreting Your Test Results

Your Score

45–50   A United States Senator from Puerto Rico will read aloud your test results for the Congressional Record in Latin.

40–44   A stained glass question mark will be placed on the tomb of the Unknown Carnival Glass Collector in a rural cemetery just outside of Winesburg, Ohio.

35–39   The manager of the convenience store in Bill's Trailer Court in Soda Springs, Kentucky, will name a carryout sandwich for you and "hold" the mustard.

30–34   The next time the NFL Super Bowl is held in Peoria, Illinois, the "Star Spangled Banner" will *not* be performed. Instead, "Fool's Paradise" will be sung in your honor.